POWERHOUSE

THE SECRETS OF CORPORATE BRANDING

BY

James R. Gregory Chairman
Tenet Partners

Copyright © 2015 Best Seller Publishing® LLC
All rights reserved. No part of this book may be used or reproduced in any manner whatsoever without prior written consent of the authors, except as provided by the United States of America copyright law.

Published by Best Seller Publishing®, Pasadena, CA Best Seller Publishing® is a registered trademark Printed in the United States of America.

ISBN-13: 978-1522901518

This publication is designed to provide accurate and authoritative information with regard to the subject matter covered. It is sold with the understanding that the publisher is not engaged in rendering legal, accounting, or other professional advice. If legal advice or other expert assistance is required, the services of a competent professional should be sought. The opinions expressed by the authors in this book are not endorsed by Best Seller Publishing® and are the sole responsibility of the author rendering the opinion.

Most Best Seller Publishing® titles are available at special quantity discounts for bulk purchases for sales promotions, premiums, fundraising, and educational use. Special versions or book excerpts can also be created to fit specific needs.

For more information, please write: Best Seller Publishing®
1346 Walnut Street, #205
Pasadena, CA 91106
or call 1(626) 765 9750
Toll Free: 1(844) 850-3500
Visit us online at: www.BestSellerPublishing.org

Praise for Powerhouse

"Jim Gregory has long been one of the most innovative thinkers in branding. I own hundreds of books on branding but Jim's books are all on my short shelf - the books to which I often refer. His ideas on branding are stimulating, practical, and are based on many years of research. I will now need to make another place on my short shelf for his most recent book - which is thought-provoking and filled with impactful ideas."

Don Sexton, Professor of Marketing, Columbia Business School, and Past-President, NY American Marketing Association (AMA)

"Gregory's Powerhouse spoke directly to me in my new role as a C.E.O. and the leadership challenges I face as the "flag bearer" for the brand. A must read for all senior executives who need metrics to track and measure corporate brand value and who struggle with hearing only the things they want to hear from their direct reports. The non-aligned insight so well explained by Jim will be a process I am installing immediately into the fabric of my organization. This book is a must read for all stakeholders in any organization".

Rick Salomone, Former 3M Executive and current Chief Executive Officer of Hologram Industries

"I've worked with Jim Gregory and his team for years — he always brings fresh ideas and strategies that can vastly improve the positioning of all brands. This book has many commonsense concepts that help build brands and drive revenue."

William A. Lafontaine, Chief Marketing Officer, Bankers Financial Corporation

"No one knows more about corporate brands than Jim Gregory, who has spent much of his life studying corporate branding. This book assembles in one place the wisdom about corporate brands that Jim has accumulated over many years. The book is a must read for marketers and

investors alike. It provides a clear roadmap for building, maintaining and evaluating corporate brands."
David W. Stewart, President's Professor of Marketing
Loyola Marymount University

"Jim Gregory has done it again with his new book: Powerhouse – The Secrets of Corporate Branding. He brings his experience and insights together in a highly readable way to guide us on how best to manage sustainable brands. It's no secret: Jim's a brand powerhouse guru!"
Donna Hamlin, Ph.D., CEO, Hamlin Harkins, Ltd.

"Corporate brands can, and should, be measured. They are one of the most valuable assets of the firm. Jim Gregory is one of the pioneers of 'Corporate Branding' and in this book he offers clear and practical guidance on how managers can build their corporate brand to offer value for the firm."
David J. Reibstein, The William S. Woodside Professor
and Professor of Marketing The Wharton School
University of Pennsylvania

"While the old adage "perception is reality" may not be applicable all the time – it certainly is true when it comes to brands. The reality is, the success of your brand in the marketplace is a direct result of how it's perceived. In "POWERHOUSE —The Secrets of Corporate Branding" you get a concise and insightful guide on the care and feeding of your brand, and the importance of ongoing research, measurement and communication. It also gives clear and implementable advice about how to grow the value of your brand and in turn improve performance in the marketplace."
Pat Redmond, President and CEO, Tervis Tumbler Company

Acknowledgements and Credits:

Special thanks to: Hampton Bridwell, Larry Oakner, Beth Flom,

Brad Puckey, Todd Powers, and the entire Tenet Partners team for contributing to segments of the book,

Becky J. Friedman for her designs and support,

Courtney Grier for the cover design and interior layout,

Matthew Porter for copywriting support, and

Charles Muir for being my consigliere on all things written.

Thanks to my friends and family who helped and encouraged me throughout the process: Evelyn Gregory, Becky Friedman, Will Gregory, David Friedman, Diane Henderson, Kent Henderson, Frank Jones, Bonnie Jones, Richard Gregory, Sally Gregory, Ed Faruolo, Blake Freeman, Linda Freeman, Susan Leggitt, Bob Matricardi and Carol E. Robbins.

Special thanks to Linda Freeman for proofreading the book.

Thanks to Kat Hughes, Editor, and Matt Walsh, Publisher, Business Observer, for permission to utilize some of the articles that I have written in their fine publication.

Thanks to Lisa Krouse for permission to shoot the cover photograph in her office building.

Thanks also to Best Seller Publishing, Inc., especially Rob Kosberg and his team — including John Ireland, Rebecca Grosch, Sydney Hubbard and Steve Fata.

This book is dedicated to
one of the world's greatest entrepreneurs:

Frederick A. DeLuca
Founder of Subway

(1948-2015)

Table of Contents

Introduction
The "Aura" Called Brand 17

CHAPTER 1

The Value of Reputation 19
Corporate Brand: A Most Valuable Asset 21

4 Cs: Clarity, Carat, Color, and Cut 21

One Gauge of Our Economy – How Strong
Is the Engine? 23

Ten Reasons Brand Value Matters 27

CHAPTER 2

Brand Leadership and the CEO 31
Resist the Status Quo while Respecting the Heritage
Accountable Leadership Starts with C-E-O 32

The CEO Is the Flag Bearer 33

What Makes an Enduring Brand? 33

CHAPTER 3

Brand Building: Every Thing You Say and Do 37
The Changing Face of Audience 37

The Corporate Brand Is the Sum of Many Parts 38

How to Transition From Commodity to Brand 39

CHAPTER 4

How to Create Differentiation 43

What Is Your USP – Unique Selling Proposition? 43

How *Differentiation* Can Put You on the Map 45

The Growth Imperative 48

How to Build a Powerful Brand... 50

CHAPTER 5

Brand Accountability 53

Beyond The CEO... 53

Board Responsibility for the Corporate Brand 54

Corporate Branding and Its Impact on
Enterprise Value 56

The Brand Is a Business Asset 56

The Brand and Stock Value 58

The Brand as a Dashboard 60

CHAPTER 6

Corporate Brand Investment: Enviable ROI 63

Reliable Metrics – Simple and Easy to Compare.............. 63

Brand 4 Cs: Coherent, Clear, and Consistent
Communications... 64

CHAPTER 7

The Benefit of Ongoing Research 67

Effective Research: What It Takes 69

Seek Non-Aligned Insight 69
Aligned Audience Viewpoints... 71
Putting Data to Work... 72

CHAPTER 8

Achieving Coherence with Brand Communications 75

Nine Steps to Effective Brand Communication 76
    Step One – Brand Strategy 76
    Step Two – The Brand Audit 77
    Step Three – Brand Architecture............................... 78
    Step Four – Brand Positioning................................... 78
    Step Five – Brand Platform 79
    Step Six – Names and Naming Systems..................... 80
    Step Seven – Identity.. 81
    Step Eight – A Unified Voice..................................... 81
    Step Nine – Brand Guidelines................................... 82

CHAPTER 9

Employee Engagement: Which Employees Build Brands Best? 85

Creating a Brand Driven Culture with Your Employees 87
Branding on the Inside is Good for Business on the Outside 88
Frustrated When Employees Ignore Directives?.............. 89

CHAPTER 10

Building an Effective Brand Council 93

Outside Consultants on the Brand Council 95

Brand Councils Work for Every Company 96

CHAPTER 11

Customer Experience as a Value Driver 97

Managing the Customer Experience 99

Delivering on the Customer Experience 99

When Does a Brand Lose Its DNA? 102

CHAPTER 12

When to Rethink the Brand 107

Refreshing Your Brand Strategy 107

When and Why Should A Company Rebrand? 109

How Should You Rebrand? 110

Respect the History and Heritage of the
Corporate Brand 110

CHAPTER 13

Social Responsibility, Social Media, and Social Listening 113

Social Listening 113

Quality Trumps Quantity in Social Media
Engagement 116

For Established Social Media Platforms and Strategies 118

Corporate Social Responsibility for Every Company 119

CHAPTER 14

Managing the Brand in a Merger 123

Merger Mania Is Heating Up 123

Brand Strategy from an M&A Perspective 123

Merging the Cultures 125

CHAPTER 15

Are Corporate Brands Relevant in Today's Economy 127

Build Your Relevance: Quantify Your Reputation Over Time 127

Sustain Your Differentiation: Understand Your Competitors 128

Raise Your Credibility: Align Your Position for a Solid Reputation 128

Leverage Your Leaders: Putting Your Management Where Your Mouth Is 129

CHAPTER 16

Building Trust 131

Truth or Consequences 131

Building "Trust Points" Into Every Business Experience 131

Celebrity Endorsements: A Good Idea Riddled With Pitfalls 133

CHAPTER 17

Entrepreneurship — Not All Brands Are Big 137

Selling Your Personal Brand 137

Renaissance of Enterprise 140

Trends to Watch 140

Enthusiasm for Global Entrepreneurism 143

So You Want to Be An Entrepreneur? 144

CHAPTER 18

My Best Advice: Clear, Concise, and Consistent Communications 147

CONCLUSION

Corporate Brand Value 151

Measure, Maintain, Nurture and Protect 151

How Do You Measure Brand Value? 151

Special Note to the Readers on Point of View:

This book is a compilation of recent articles, white papers, blogs, and original writing just for the book – all with the purpose of sharing my thoughts on the most important concepts around corporate branding. There is an inconsistency about whether the writer is speaking directly to the reader, or whether it is Tenet or someone else speaking to the reader. I didn't correct this simply because I believe the context of each concept is clear. I feel the readers will understand the differences. If this is annoying, please let me know, and I'll address it in subsequent editions.

INTRODUCTION:

The "Aura" Called "Brand"

Whether you sell apples or Apples, attitude or Dell, caramel-flavored fizzy water or Coca-Cola, a company is only as valuable as its brand is desirable. Inventing and manufacturing a product is hard work. Getting people to try it, buy it, and want more of it is even harder. Protecting the aura, which has been carefully crafted to protect the brand that surrounds it, is hardest of all.

"Brand" is not a product. It is an intangible perception — a feeling — about a product, service, or company, a feeling shared by a group of individuals. Everything you do — *everything* — can shape that feeling or color that aura. Consciously building the corporate brand includes everything from the quality and precision of your R&D to the ethics and integrity of your manufacture, from the delivery of your product to their doorstep to the intelligence and responsiveness of your retail sales representative at the shopping mall, from the strength of the shipping container to the recycled content of the packaging inside it, and from the color and concept behind the logotype to the user experience on your website. That is why it is so important to think about your corporate brand holistically.

Your corporate brand is the sum of everything you say and do about your product, service, or company and the reality of how well your product, service, or company delivers on its promise. That feeling, or aura, around the brand has tremendous value that can be measured and managed like other business assets in the company. It creates a premium value for both your products and your stock price (enterprise value if you are not a public company).

So just to be clear, this book does not focus on product or service brands. It is about corporate brands. To most outsiders, your corporate brand is your company, a distillation of factors such as name recognition, reputation, and economic value that determine whether they will invest in your company, buy its products, and recognize and repeat its name.

This book is about managing corporate brands to increase their value. If management wants to build enterprise value, it requires the dedication, focus, commitment and consistency of management. It need not be complex if the will to do it exists in the hearts and minds of those men and women at the pinnacle of any company or organization.

This book is also about the leadership required to build and maintain brilliant corporate brands. Great corporate brands require visionary leaders willing to take risks that allow the brands to stand for more than utility. These leaders make brands embodiments of the company's ethos and customer satisfaction.

About Tenet Partners

Tenet Partners stands at the forefront of brand valuation and brand strategy. In the pages that follow, we share some of our trade secrets on how to maintain and build strong brands of great value, which are one of a corporation's most valuable assets. For further information on Tenet Partners, please visit our website TenetPartners.com or contact me directly at jgregory@tenetpartners.com or 203-979-7914.

CHAPTER 1

The Value of Reputation

"A good reputation is more valuable than money."
~ PUBLILIUS SYRUS, MAXIM 108

Today, when it comes to your company's reputation, which audience matters most? Customers? Employees? Investors? Media? The correct answer is that they all matter because any individual from any one of these audiences can have a huge and immediate impact on the reputation of your company.

For Publilius Syrus, his reputation was indeed more valuable than money. It was the difference between slavery and freedom. His story is as interesting as the maxims he wrote. In the first century BC, he was a Syrian slave brought to Italy. He earned his freedom the old-fashioned way – by humoring his master with his intelligence. What is known of him today is a series of one-sentence maxims of which number 108 is my personal favorite, "A good reputation is more valuable than money." For business, the concepts are the same, but the scale is somewhat different.

Think of the damage caused to a company's reputation when a critical blog post becomes viral. One example is the customer who recorded a FedEx driver throwing a computer monitor over a fence and posted it to YouTube. Remember it? The video went viral overnight. When most companies would have gone to the bunkers, FedEx responded quickly and aggressively. They responded in like fashion on YouTube with a FedEx spokesman who expressed his personal outrage at this unacceptable behavior by a FedEx employee, and they did it while maintaining the employee's privacy. They met with the customer and solved the issue to the customer's satisfaction. FedEx reached multiple audiences simultaneously with a highly focused response. The crisis was quickly acknowledged, addressed, and arbitrated.

Think about all the audiences that are most important to your business. Of these, which are the most critical audiences to your business today? Do you know how these critical audiences feel about your company? Are those perceptions changing over time? Are there new dynamics at play with the potential to impact your brand? Are there new competitors in your marketplace? Are competitors introducing new products before you can react? How is the economy impacting your business?

Are you vulnerable to a viral-type crisis? Do you have a crisis recovery plan in place?

One way to keep your finger on the pulse of your reputation is by conducting annual benchmark tracking research with all of your critical audiences and against all of your major competitors. Brand tracking market research will help you see how reputation dynamics can change over time and how changing market conditions and events both within and outside of your control impact them.

This intelligence will provide you with insights, allowing you to prioritize your audiences and adjust your messages so your communication has the most impact. When you focus a highly targeted message on a specific audience, you have the best chance of having a positive result – whether the goal is to generate more revenue, get Wall Street to support your stock price, or simply bolster your corporate reputation.

Prioritizing your audiences to give your communications the most focused impact at the right time is how your message can break through the clutter of all the competitors who are also communicating at the same time.

So what are the business lessons to be learned from Publilius Syrus? By knowing his most important audience, and by focusing on convincing his master that he was worthy of special attention and treatment, Publilius Syrus was able to get the master to take dramatic and highly unusual action that made all of the other successes in his life possible. Knowing your audience and focusing your message can move mountains.

Corporate Brand: A Most Valuable Asset

The corporate brand is your company's most valuable asset. Indeed, to outsiders, it is your company. Your corporate brand is a distillation of factors such as name recognition, reputation, and economic value that determine whether individuals will invest in your company, buy its products, and recognize and repeat its name.

While *brand value* is an *intangible asset* failure to recognize the precision with which a company's foremost asset can be calculated; will inevitably lead to a missed opportunity to maximize that value. Corporate brands, like diamonds, can be measured and weighed – and, therefore, shaped, valued, and managed for even greater value.

4 CS: Clarity, Carat, Color, and Cut

The analogy of comparing brands to rare gems makes a lot of sense. The value of both brands and diamonds can vary widely if there are not clear measurement standards in place to evaluate the many potentially subjective perceptions. A large diamond may not be worth nearly as much as a small, high-quality one. If there are not standards in place, the public could be duped on the actual value of the larger diamond. The precision of standards to evaluate corporate value is crucial to company success. Corporate leaders, like the diamond industry, prosper when using a scientific method for grading the quality of their gems.

Consider this: Gemological Institute of America (GIA) certifies diamonds based on the "4 Cs": *Clarity, Carat, Color, and Cut.* These measures level the playing field so diamond buyers understand the basis of their stone's value – and sellers can act accordingly. Buyers who understand the value of diamonds make confident purchases, and companies that understand the value of their corporate and product brands know best how to market, insure, sell, and trade. The difference between a badly managed brand and a legendary one is the difference between a stone and a diamond. The core of building brands is building enterprise value – what we call "Corporate Capital."

Like a diamond, the best brands sparkle and shine, drawing attention, admiration, and – sometimes – envy. While color, carat, clarity, and cut are the 4 Cs of the gem industry, companies may be measured by these six indices: familiarity, coherence, favorability, reputation, leadership, and investment worthiness.

FAMILIARITY (RECOGNITION) – How well is your brand recognized by key constituents?

COHERENCE – How clearly is your brand resonating with your key constituencies?

FAVORABILITY – Do others recognize your brand's breadth and depth? Is that perception an accurate reflection of your brand's whole story?

REPUTATION – What do others think of your company's human resources, products, and services?

LEADERSHIP – How do key constituents view the quality of your corporate and brand leadership? Do they view its leadership as transparent and accountable? Do they respect its integrity? Do they admire its operation and vision?

INVESTMENT WORTHINESS – Does the financial community view your corporation and its brands as appealing investments?

Brilliant brands are not created by desire alone. If only wishing could make it so, every cola company would as successful as The Coca-Cola Company. Like cutting a diamond, crafting a brand takes great effort and specialized knowledge. It requires vision, planning, stamina, patience, and money well spent.

One Gauge of Our Economy – How Strong Is the Engine?

CoreBrand has been engaged since 1990 in continuously monitoring the reputations of 1,000 companies across fifty industries . This study, collectively known as the CoreBrand® Index, is unique in that is it the only continuous examination of the corporate brand as a contributor to enterprise value. Thus, the study is a fair reflection of corporate enterprise value and its impact on the US and even the global economy.

The growth of intangible assets as a contributor to the economy is undeniable. In 1975, intangible assets such as brands accounted for under twenty percent of the total market cap of most companies. Today, the contribution of intangible assets is over eighty percent. Yet internally grown intangible assets are not on the balance sheet. Therefore, they are not represented or accounted for as drivers of the economy.

Recognizing this accounting shortfall, CoreBrand created a research method and analytical model to determine brand equity and value as the brand grows or shrinks over time. It does so by quantitatively determining the following:

1) the percentage of the company's market cap that is attributable directly to its corporate brand

2) the translation into a dollar value percentage of market cap attributable to the brand

The following charts examine the CoreBrand 500 and the CoreBrand 100 companies. These represent the biggest and best-known companies in the world. By looking at the averages consistently over time, we can examine and help evaluate the health of the economy.

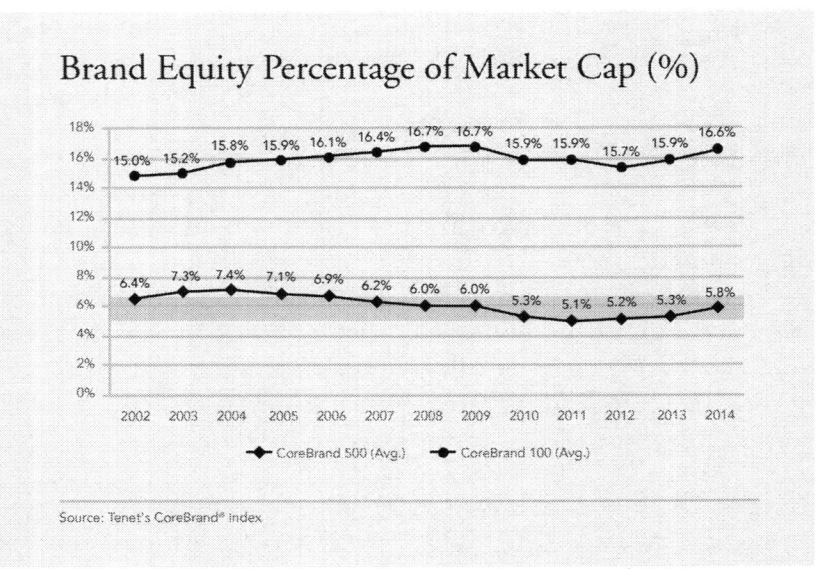

Source: Tenet's CoreBrand® Index

The CoreBrand 500 average range of contribution to market cap is five to seven percent. Over the past decade, there has been a steady decline in the CoreBrand 500 average, dropping from a high of 7.4 percent in 2004 down to 5.1 percent in 2011 and remaining stuck at that lower level. This is a fair reflection of a lethargic economy recovery. It basically indicates that the economy is not being driven by business.

The CoreBrand 100, which consists of corporations with the strongest corporate brands, fared better longer, with the downward inflection point coming in 2009 and having less than a one percent negative impact on total enterprise value. The CoreBrand 100 average stayed within the fifteen to seventeen percent range over the past decade. Interestingly, this elite group continued to grow from 2004 to 2009 before declining. The lesson is that big brands hold their value longer and enjoy a brand premium value eight to ten percent above the broader CoreBrand 500.

Why did the CoreBrand 500 begin to decline in 2004 while the CoreBrand 100 continued to improve until 2008? We believe it was due to the Sarbanes-Oxley Act becoming the law of the land in

2002. As it was being implemented, the law was seen by the survey respondents of business leaders to be a greater burden on the mid-sized rather than the biggest companies.

It was probably not the intent of the framers of the "SOX" law to unduly punish the mid-size companies. It is interesting to observe, however, the averages between the CoreBrand 100 and the CoreBrand 500. 2003's average percentages show the smallest gap – 7.9 percent – between the Top 100 and Top 500. Conversely, the largest gap between the Top 100 and Top 500, a gap of 10.7 percent, was in 2008. This is significant when even a single percent can represent hundreds of millions or even billions of dollars of market value. Another point of interest in the data is that 2003 shows the Top 100 having twice the equity as the Top 500. 2014 shows the Top 100 having tripled the equity of the Top 500.

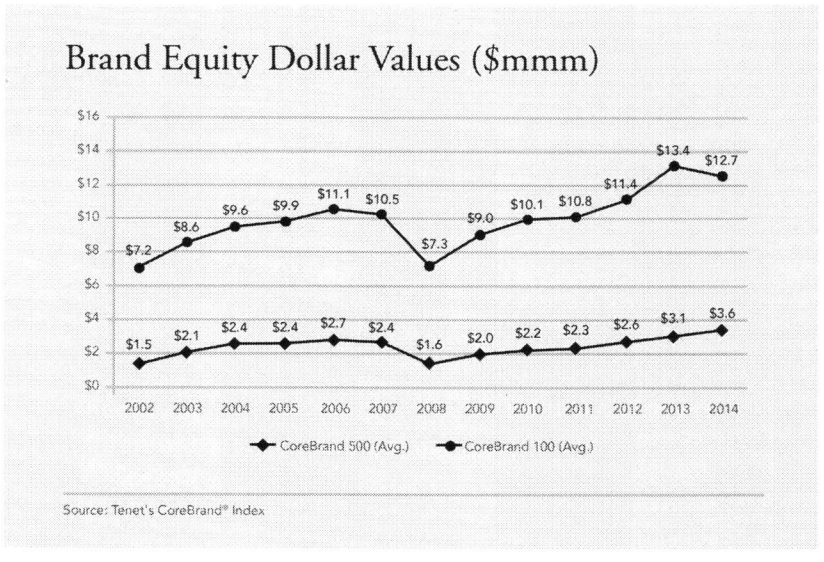

The CoreBrand 500 brand equity market value ranges from $1.5-$3.1 billion over the past twelve years, with 2008 taking the biggest hit. The CoreBrand 100 also took the hardest hit in 2008, with an average loss of $3.2 billion, but these top performing companies only took two years to recoup that loss, and they have now peaked at 16.6% or $12.7 billion.

How was the CoreBrand 100 able to recoup since 2008 so much brand equity value while the brand equity as a percentage of market cap, which is a value driver, remained relatively flat? Quite simply, the general economy was slowly improving due to the economic stimulus package and low interest rates over that timeframe. The corporate brand didn't play as much of a role as a value driver as it has in past economic recoveries.

Basically, this means the economy is not firing on all cylinders. The recovery we are experiencing, while not entirely bad, is not entirely healthy. When brand equity scores improve as a fundamental value driver, you will know that the economy is more balanced and will be self-sustaining with less requirement for artificial stimulus and government-mandated low interest rates.

> **THAT MOST VALUABLE ASSET**
>
> Tenet's CoreBrand Index® (CBI) analysis indicates that corporate brand equity for the "CoreBrand 500" companies represents, on average, five to seven percent of total market capitalization. This percentage represents an average $2-3 billion in value for each company in this group. The "CoreBrand 100" generates an even greater portion of the total value of the company from its corporate brand. These elite corporate brands represent fifteen to seventeen percent of market cap for their companies on average and $13 billion in brand equity value. This represents a formidable asset in any of these companies.
>
> Brand equity varies significantly from industry to industry. For example, among the building material industry players, CBI analysis indicates that corporate brand value has a relatively low impact of two percent on total market capitalization. On the other hand, in the beverage industry, corporate brand has a major impact of eleven percent on total market capitalization.

> End user customers care a lot about the brand of soft drink they put in their mouths but not so much about the brand of plywood they use in their homes. So long as Lowe's or Home Depot stands behind it, consumers are satisfied. The same is not true for B2B buyers. Their brand interests can be far more detailed and nuanced.

Ten Reasons Brand Value Matters

The corporate brand is probably the least understood asset in most companies, yet it can be one of the greatest tools the CEO can use to build enterprise value described earlier as Corporate Capital.

Here are ten good reasons why CEOs should pay close attention to corporate brand valuation and to nurturing it and viewing it as a long-term growth asset:

#1 Brand Valuation legitimizes investment. — When you understand and define the value that the brand creates, questions about brand-building investments change from "whether or not to invest" to "how much to invest." Companies that understand the value manage their brand investment to maintain and maximize the corporate capital being created. These companies are characterized by communicating aggressively to shape the landscape of their markets, thus managing their markets to their strengths and reaping the associated benefits.

#2 Brand Valuation provides an objective measure of effort. — By measuring the impact of brand building, leadership can evaluate the quality of branding efforts without resorting to subjective opinions or personal perspective. Measurement and metrics add science to the art of creative brand building.

#3 Brand Valuation creates accountability. — By utilizing a tangible measure of impact, leadership and marketing teams can be evaluated by their stewardship and management using a tangible asset over the long term.

#4 Brand Valuation aligns leadership. — Creating a common vocabulary for a brand gives marketing an appropriate seat at the management table. Because the return for branding can be identified and tracked over time, the effort and return for any department is visible. This allows all senior managers to work together for the optimum total return on investment. When finance and marketing cooperate, working toward defined goals, everyone wins.

#5 Brand Valuation identifies growth opportunities. — Understanding brand value illustrates the opportunity to advance a business not only through geographical growth but also through product and service adjacencies.

#6 Brand Valuation predicts market shifts. — By understanding the relationship between brand value and other performance drivers, leadership can identify changing market conditions. Intelligence is about understanding where the market is going before your competitors know. This is usually best done by knowing the right questions to ask, by researching continuously, and by creating custom models that zealously seek the answers.

#7 Brand Valuation identifies competitive opportunity and advantage. Understanding brand value relative to competitors can drive changes in market-growth strategies. By interpreting the value of your brand vs. competitors and the dimensions that drive that value, you gain valuable intelligence for creating and maintaining a competitive market advantage in the areas that define business success. Discerning the market and opportunity available can point a company in the right direction.

#8 Brand Valuation informs M&A or strategic alliances. — Understanding the value of all business assets will enhance negotiations in mergers, acquisitions, and partnerships. M&A can be tricky, and emotional attachment to pre-existing entities can be strong. But by understanding the value and dimension of all brands involved, leadership can strategically deploy those brands for maximum impact.

#9 Brand Valuation creates licensing opportunities. — Understanding the brand's value permits predictable revenue growth through licensing efforts. A brand on the move creates momentum that can be leveraged and licensing is a great way to make significant income from the brand itself.

#10 Brand Valuation helps define the value of other intangibles. — Is it good business to be a good corporate citizen? Sustainable business practices, Corporate Social Responsibility (CSR), philanthropy, and other "goodwill" efforts can be understood and valued. Knowing the amount of impact can help make CSR a good business decision rather than one based purely on the goodness of the management of the company.

Brand Valuation begins with consistently benchmark tracking the brands vital to your growth. There are many valuation experts – including your accounting firm – who can help you set a value for your brand. Your brand is what sets you apart from your competition. Always remember that measuring, valuing, and managing the corporate brand and your product brands is a key component of managing the financial health of the corporation.

CHAPTER 2

Brand Leadership and the CEO

We like to think that a great CEO has steel in his or her veins, but there are many other qualities associated with a great leader, such as the ability to delegate and to inspire confidence. Other essential qualities are trustworthiness, visionary leadership, financial acuity, and the ability to communicate clearly. Of all these qualities, the most important is the ability to communicate. Communication is a tool by which all other qualities are distributed. The distribution system is called "corporate branding," and a CEO who masters that is a true leader.

A great CEO has brand foresight. While many great ideas come from below, the most famous and admirable brand strategies start at the top. Leaders of enormous vision and enthusiasm are willing to take calculated risks and allow their brands to stand for more than utility. A brand is *more* than a soft drink. A brand is *more* than a car. A brand is *more* than a jet engine. It has to be a pause that refreshes, the ultimate driving machine, or imagination at work. These are not just empty slogans – they represent the core values that companies and their leaders were willing to stake out and claim.

Creating a brilliant corporate brand requires leaders with strong will and courage. The CEO must have the foresight to actively communicate the brand's strengths to every key audience, which includes customers, employees, investors, and the board of directors. Each audience represents one facet of the brand's overall strength, and the CEO must ensure each is well-managed and carefully articulated.

Resist the Status Quo While Respecting the Heritage

Without a strong sense of mission and the courage to sustain it no CEO alone is equipped to handle the complexities of growth management. Leading a company to brand brilliance requires great imagination, forward thinking, and a willingness to jettison an outdated philosophy and the complacency of past successes. A true leader is never satisfied with the status quo. Brands constantly move, grow, adapt, and respond – or fade into mediocrity. But the inherent motivation to build a new brand needs to be balanced with an understanding and respect for the heritage from which the underlying brand equity comes. That balancing act is what separates the merely good leaders from the great ones.

Great leaders make their brands extensions of themselves; they embody the spirit of the company and make customer satisfaction with their products a personal mission. They impart their enthusiasm and commitment to the brand across the entire enterprise – from the boardroom to the executive suite, from the production floor to the delivery door, from the salesperson to the end user. With this dedication, their brands can become icons such as Coke, Apple, Virgin, Ben & Jerry's, Macy's, Ford, Amazon, Google, Starbucks, and of course, Berkshire Hathaway.

Accountable Leadership Starts with C-E-O

The CEO must monitor the corporate brand for strength, weakness, and any opportunity for change that could positively (or negatively) affect corporate health and vitality of the company.

The board should tie the CEO's compensation to the growth of the corporate brand because it is such a bellwether of the company, and it impacts so many aspects of the company's performance. The CEO should report each quarter to the board about the corporate brand.

Despite the corporate brand's being an intangible asset, the CEO should encourage and embrace its valuation to understand the financial importance of this growth generator.

The CEO should evaluate marketing communications budgets based on the potential ROI and according to the company's long-term goals and the vitality of the corporate brand.

In order to continuously guide long-term strategic planning, the CEO must have empirical data and insights into industry, technology, and consumer preferences that affect brand strength and/or brand equity.

The CEO must hold his senior management team accountable for exhibiting the same high level of commitment to the corporate brand.

The CEO is the Flag Bearer

Like it or not, the CEO is the brand's chief flag bearer. A short-term attitude will not make for a brand of enduring strength. Brilliant brands require long-term commitment to investment and change. Great CEOs know this and invest accordingly. They are ardent champions of constant growth and gradual change. They encourage operational improvement and direct corporate restructuring *before* outside forces such as technological advancement and consumer evolution leave them in the dust. They are at the vanguard of industry change, and they invest the capital and time needed to ensure that their brands remain at the forefront.

What Makes an Enduring Brand?

There are many wonderful examples of marketing successes. The essence of brand building is endurance that translates into value creation. Listed below are five of the most enduring brands. What lessons can we learn for application in our own businesses?

TIFFANY – The blue box – Perhaps no other box has created more excitement and delight than the iconic Tiffany blue box with the white ribbon. According to the Tiffany Co. website, Charles Lewis Tiffany mandated that the coveted boxes could only be acquired with a Tiffany purchase. As reported by the *New York Sun* in 1906,

"Tiffany has one thing in stock that you cannot buy off him for as much money as you may offer, he will only give it to you. And that is one of his boxes." The brand lesson is exclusive packaging tied to a powerful experience. Glimpsed on a busy street or resting in the palm of a hand, Tiffany blue boxes make hearts beat faster and epitomize Tiffany's great heritage of elegance, exclusivity, and flawless craftsmanship.

THE COCA-COLA COMPANY – The contoured bottle recently celebrated its 100th birthday. This proves a point that not all enduring brands are about packaging an expensive experience. As my colleague, Russ Napolitano, said in a recent blog on the subject, "What foresight the marketers and packaging engineers and designers had in creating such a bottle and to have it patented no less."

BURBERRY – The classic checkered pattern – How does a coat lining become an enduring brand? This one is as interesting as it is puzzling. It is simply a fabric design made of woven Scottish cashmere. When did it transcend from a coat lining to a design icon representing quality? First, it was distinctive and yet understated – as a trench coat lining, it wasn't highly visible – yet you always knew it was an original if you could get a glimpse of the lining. It remained consistent over time. Then, when applied to products such as scarves, umbrellas, and purses, the plaid became a standalone classic.

CADILLAC – Reinventing luxury while reintroducing quality – The Cadillac brand has been under pressure for decades from the highly engineered German luxury imports. With so many luxury cars sold in the United States, why couldn't America make a luxury car worthy of competing on the global stage? In recent years, they have. The Cadillac brand has made a comeback starting around 2000. It began with a recommitment to design, quality, and performance. Today's Cadillac is well-engineered and fun to drive. It's comfortable without being the flying sofa of less spirited decades.

HARLEY-DAVIDSON – Another reinvented icon tied to a cultural experience — Left for dead as brand in the 1970s, the company was purchased in 1981 from a holding company by a group of diehard enthusiast investors who believed in the brand and believed it could roar back to become once again one of America's great brands. The new management team reintroduced a retro design of earlier models while recommitting to high-quality manufacturing. It worked, and customers returned. Over the next thirty-five years, their brand has surged ahead from the back of the CoreBrand Index® reputation measurement study to become one of its most consistent top brands. Today, Harley-Davidson maintains a consistently well-managed brand from the sound of its engine, to the logo, to the culture. The company enjoys a huge brand following, which they nurture carefully through clubs, events, and even museums. This perpetuates licensing opportunities and significant revenue.

Were these brands originally developed to become enduring brands? Not always. Sometimes longevity itself is the reason – stick around long enough and you'll have a following. The trick to harvesting the value of an enduring brand is careful management.

A brand becomes a candidate for endurance when the experience between the product and the customer transcends the expected. Enduring brands provide not only a reliable experience, but also an aura of expectation beyond the product functionality. What is your favorite enduring brand? What are the qualities that make it stand the test of time?

MANAGING BRANDS FOR ENDURANCE — DO'S AND DON'TS

DO – Provide a consistent customer experience over time

DON'T – Be all things to all people – focus on the customer experience

DO – Respect and protect the heritage of your brand

DON'T – Be afraid to refresh and reinvigorate brands that have lost momentum

DO – Conduct consistently research among your customers

DON'T – Over license your brand – It's a quick way to kill exclusivity.

DO – Have a tactile component to your brand experience – From the Harley roar to the Coke bottle shape, most enduring brands combine the visual with the other senses.

DON'T – Use endorsements without thinking about the consequences of failure

DO – Feel confident about charging slightly more for enduring brands

DON'T – Sell yourself short. Discounting is one of the quickest ways to kill a premium brand.

CHAPTER 3

Brand Building: Everything You Say and Do

It is easy to confuse a corporate brand with a corporate reputation. While your brand is a goal, reputation is a means to your goal. Corporate reputation is the sum of all the impressions your corporation makes with its key constituents. A good reputation includes recognition that your management is transparent and accountable. Corporate branding is the strategy that oversees those actions – it is the process of consciously and strategically building your corporate reputation through everything you say and do. If an action or statement can be linked to your business, it impacts your reputation. Consequently, you must evaluate how every action, internally or externally, influences the perception of your company, and that is done through corporate branding.

The Changing Face of Audience

Your corporate brand should reflect every facet of your business. Your brand *strategy* should drive your corporate culture and the business processes associated with each of your key constituencies. To effectively manage your corporate brand you must clearly, concisely, and consistently communicate the interests of your most vital audiences and other constituents. Who are they? They can be one group, but tomorrow, quite another. The fact is, as tastes, needs, and technologies change, so do audiences. Your success will be measured by the relevancy of the brand to their lives. The following groups are typical of those followed by most companies:

- Customers
- Employees
- Government officials
- Local communities
- Management teams
- Media

- Shareholders
- Financial analysts
- Investor activists
- Any others critical to success

It is virtually impossible to serve these diverse audiences simultaneously. For example, communications directed to employees will be different from those aimed at shareholders so you must prioritize in order to maintain relationships with those who are most important to your corporate reputation and brand health.

Once you have determined which constituents are vital to your long-term growth, it is essential to periodically measure their familiarity with and understanding of your brand. Quantifiable, periodic measurement will allow you to understand your constituents' needs and create strategies and processes to satisfy them. However, do not forget your lower profile constituencies. Every audience you have listed that is important to your success should be evaluated once a year to determine whether it's time to benchmark its attitudes toward the company. You never want to be caught without a basic understanding and tracking system of those audiences critical to your company. Do they see you as a run of the mill commodity, or do they truly understand what sets you apart?

The Corporate Brand is the Sum of Many Parts

How does the brand look from the CEO's office or boardroom? This graphic shows how all brands, while unique, are comprised of four fundamental elements.

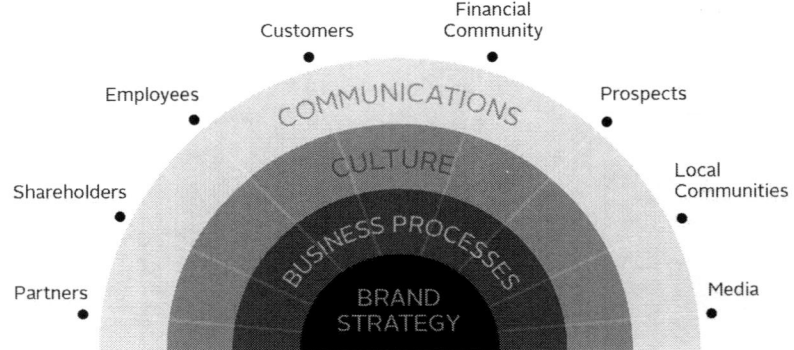

#1 CORE BRAND: The brand strategy, vision, or value upon which the company was founded and which drives its operations.

#2 BUSINESS PROCESS: The processes and systems that make the company profitable. These include any process used to develop, to build the market, and to deliver products or services the company sells for profit.

#3 CULTURE: The ethos of your corporation; its collective character. Culture is cumulative and can be volatile (the "one bad apple" syndrome). Subcultures threaten the consistency of the culture. Internal-brand training is vital.

#4 COMMUNICATIONS: Everything we say and do that impacts brand (Familiarity, Coherence, and Reputation). This includes highly intentional public communication (advertising, packaging, PR) and unintentional communications such as overheard speech, errant emails, or ill-advised social media postings.

How to Transition from Commodity to Brand

NEVER BE A COMMODITY

There is no product that is more of a commodity than salt, a simple chemical compound. Morton Salt, celebrating its 100th birthday this year, created the Morton Salt Girl along with the tagline "When It Rains It Pours®" and launched it in a national advertising campaign to illustrate that Morton salt would flow freely even in damp weather. Morton became a brand and enjoyed preference and premium pricing for one hundred years over all other salt products.

Years ago, I owned a firm in the creative services industry, which was exciting except there were so many other creative service vendors that we were perceived as one of many. Despite being in a highly creative business, there was a point where my own company was thought of as a commodity. To generate business, we were forced to go hat-in-hand to prospective clients seeking any work available rather than pitching in areas where we excelled. We were sure that our work was as good if not better than any competitor, but the perception others had of us was our reality.

The result of being a commodity is a downward pressure on pricing until you can no longer make a profit. When we did land a piece of business, the fee was so low that we didn't feel like being very creative. When this happens, you must find a way to leverage your talents and build on your strengths to improve the price of your product and the public perception of your firm.

CREATE THE STRATEGY

When we were perceived as a commodity, I determined to make three strategic changes:

1) I wanted to break out of the perception of being a local business.

2) I wanted our services to be in demand on a global basis.

3) I wanted to charge a premium price for our creativity.

FIND YOUR EXPERTISE

Find something you really love within the field you have chosen. I chose advertising and then chose the specialty of corporate branding because I felt I could move mountains by helping CEOs brand their company. I would be differentiated in the industry.

BECOME AN EXPERT – WRITE A BOOK

I really knew my business, but not everyone knew that I knew my business. When my first book was published, I instantly had expert credentials in my field. Why? Because I wrote the book, and it differentiated my business from any others. It was a turning point in my career.

HOW QUICKLY WILL CHANGE HAPPEN?

Changes begin as soon as you develop a strategy because you begin to think differently about everything from your sales pitch to your own personal brand. After my book was published, a total internal transformation happened, and within three years, my company had completely changed our model for business. You, too, should be able to see progress toward your goals within six months from the time you begin to implement the plan.

MEASURING PROGRESS

It's hard to see progress when you are embroiled in the day-to-day battle to succeed, but if you examine periodically your successes (every six months), you should be able to see a pattern of growth that can't be denied. Benchmarking consistently through research or other specific measures will tell you how far you've improved during that time. The most obvious benchmark is revenue, but you can also benchmark the number of times your company is mentioned in the media, the numbers of employees who are hired, new customers who are acquired, etc. Take the time to reflect and to celebrate your progress.

THE IMPORTANT THING IS TO STAY THE COURSE

There are a thousand reasons to back away from a strategy. It is often easier to retrench to the old ways of doing business simply because they are familiar. But you will never achieve the levels of success that staying on the new course will give you.

LEVERAGE YOUR SUCCESS

Make sure that achieving your goals leads to new goals. When I wrote my first book, it was the accomplishment of a huge goal. I could have coasted for years, but instead, I saw that it opened up new business opportunities I hadn't previously anticipated. I immediately started my second book. Taking advantage of your accomplishments is as important as achieving them.

BEING AN EXPERT CREATES AN EXPECTATION

It's not always what you are an expert in that helps your business grow. Sometimes just being the best in your particular area leads to other opportunities. For example, we have a particular expertise in measuring ROI for advertising and communications investment. Quite often, we get unrelated assignments simply because we understand ROI. Prospective customers make their own connections and have their own rationale for hiring you, but you need to be ready to move when called upon.

NEVER REST ON YOUR LAURELS

With The Morton Girl now over a hundred years old, the company has announced plans to reinvigorate the brand. They have done so carefully and with great respect to the heritage of the brand, but their focus is on the next hundred years.

CHAPTER 4

How to Create Differentiation

What is Your USP – Unique Selling Proposition?

One of the great "got it" moments of my career was when I first heard the phrase "Unique Selling Proposition" (USP). Rosser Reeves was a true *Mad Men* advertising icon whose accomplishments were used to model the television character, Don Draper. Mr. Reeves wrote a book in the early 1960s called *Reality in Advertising*, which is still in print and as relevant as ever. In the book, he identifies a reasonably easy way to differentiate your business, and he coined the phrase Unique Selling Proposition to describe it.

Every company needs a USP to succeed in business. It is the one special thing about your company, service, or product that sets you apart from all of your competitors. Your USP should be differentiating and not easily duplicated by your competitors. Your USP should be promoted and advertised – ultimately becoming the cornerstone of your brand-building efforts.

How do you know that you have a unique selling proposition? Every company has one. It's a matter of uncovering it, discovering it, or inventing it if you feel that your company is a commodity without differentiation. It's the thing that customers really like about you. It's what keeps them coming back instead of going to your competitors.

However, your unique selling proposition isn't always obvious. It sometimes needs to be teased out of the myriad features and benefits that your business offers. It generally goes beyond products and services to identify a way of doing business – a closely held belief or a "tenet" so to speak.

Another way of looking at your USP is that it is your entire sales pitch summarized in a single sentence or thought. It is the proverbial elevator speech, but faster and boiled down to something you would say to a sales prospect as the doors to the elevator are closing. What would you say? What one sentence would clinch the sale? How do you create a USP that both sells your company and conveys your differentiating essence?

There is no universal answer. It takes the serious work of thinking about your brand to identify an exceptional USP, so here are six steps I use to start the process with clients:

#1 KNOW YOUR CUSTOMERS – First and foremost, it is important to know your customers and how they perceive your brand. Ask them what makes your brand unique. Ask them why they come back to you. Maybe you already have a USP, but it needs to be communicated more clearly.

#2 KNOW YOUR ENVIRONMENT – Take a fresh look at your competitive position in the marketplace. Who are your toughest competitors? How are they positioned, and what brand space do they own? What is their unique selling proposition? How are you going to differentiate your brand from theirs?

#3 DISRUPT YOUR INDUSTRY – Every industry has areas that need to be reinvented and revitalized. If you aren't positioned to be the disrupter, you will most assuredly become the disrupted at some point. Make sure your USP is on the leading edge and not trailing the change in your industry.

#4 EMBRACE THE VISION – If you have a vision of the future for the company and industry, take a fresh look at how that vision can be embodied in a USP.

#5 WRITE THEM DOWN – Revisit your USP candidates daily for a week. Get feedback from trusted management members. Narrow the list. Have your top management team vote on them. Make a decision on the one that will have the greatest positive long-term impact on the company.

#6 CODIFY THE USP INTO A BRAND STRATEGY – Once you have the USP, you must then refine it into a brand message and incorporate it into the brand strategy, making sure it is communicated throughout the organization. These precious words will ultimately become your driving force for growth.

Remember, your USP should not be confused with a tagline. A tagline, when it really works well, is a beacon that sends a message to all of the key constituencies of the company about the essence of the corporate brand – including all of the products and services under the corporate umbrella.

BMW's timeless "The Ultimate Driving Machine" tagline was created to give the impression that BMW is a car that has been engineered for *you*, the driver.

The tagline is succinct and punchy. It keeps the brand promise, but the USP is the deal closer.

Developing a USP is an old-fashioned marketing tradition that has withstood the test of time as one of the most effective exercises you can utilize to differentiate your company in the marketplace.

How Differentiation Can Put You on the Map

I'm always surprised when I hear someone say, "I can't afford to build my brand." I think in most cases these individuals are confused about what branding really means. Branding isn't always about big, flashy advertising campaigns. It's about creating differentiation from your competitors. Every company has a brand. Whether or not you choose to manage your brand, however, can be the difference between success and failure in business.

Small companies often have a greater need for branding as a competitive advantage than the big companies who generally already have well-established brands. Branding is about everything you say and do in all forms of communications, whether planned or not. Therefore, managing your brand should be embedded in your culture and business processes.

Google built its brand by word of mouth. They didn't do any advertising until fairly recently when the brand was already well-established. In fact, I remember giving a speech many years ago and mentioning that Google was this interesting new startup that everyone should pay attention to because it had a great business concept. In the audience was Kendra DiGirolamo, one of the company's very first employees, who handed me a Google tee shirt as a thank you for mentioning Google. Looking back, I should have had her sign and date it.

Of course, not every company is a budding Google. Sometimes the more mundane your company or undifferentiated your industry, the greater the opportunity exists for branding. Using the example of Morton Salt, let's again consider that every grain of salt is chemically the same as any other grain. Talk about a commodity. Yet Morton made their salt into a brand with the now-famous tagline, "When it rains it pours." They created a perception of differentiation that solved a consumer problem – the clogging of salt in damp weather. They also created a catchy little jingle that still plays in my mind. It has no real meaning, but it becomes a mantra when it's heard repeatedly, "No salt salts, like Morton salt salts." A brilliant concept simply executed.

One of my favorite small brands is a veterinary clinic called South Salem Animal Hospital in South Salem, New York. New owners purchased the business and immediately realized that their location, while on a fairly busy highway, was not very visible. They also had many competitors in the area. Previous owners of the property had left behind two large cement sculptures of dogs – about the size of Dobermans – which were soon to be heading to the dump. On a whim, instead of discarding them, the new owners began dressing up the dogs to reflect the seasons. At first, it was Thanksgiving, and they were dressed as Pilgrims. Then at Christmas, they were dressed as the Mr. & Mrs. Claus. At Easter, they were dressed as Easter bunnies. Every time we passed South Salem Animal Hospital, my kids went wild wondering how the dogs would be dressed. Cars began to pull over to take pictures. The theme grew – and soon local football teams were represented. Proms were celebrated with the dogs in a tuxedo and a gown. Great fun. And totally differentiating. Articles began to appear in the local press. It was great for business, and it cost next to nothing to execute while putting a hard-to-find location on the map.

Another commodity industry is polyethylene pipe – if you've seen one black pipe, you've seen them all. But one manufacturer put a green stripe along the length of their pipe, and this changed the industry. Suddenly, everyone knew the pipe with the green stripe. The green line took on a life of its own without adding any inherent value whatsoever. When the pipe was used in construction, the green lines were often aligned by workers even though there was no meaning or value in doing so. The stripe created an aura of differentiation. It cost nothing to paint the green line, but the premium value of the green line grew – customers demanded it. It changed the industry. Brilliant.

Nothing beats differentiation for beating the competition. So how does one differentiate? It's a process of thinking about your brand from a fresh perspective. Ask yourself:

How does your competition position their company?
_____

What position does your competition own?
_____

What assets do you have that make you unique?
_____

What is your company's greatest strength?
_____

Can you own it? Is it differentiated?
_____

What position can you own?

Will it help you gain a competitive advantage?

Is your desired position usable over the long term?

Going through this exercise and developing perceptual maps of where you are and where you want to be over a set period of time is the first step in creating a differentiated positioning. It is also the first step in branding. Creating a differentiated brand will often mean the difference between success and failure. And always remember that you don't need to outspend the competition. It's all about leveraging what makes you different from them.

The Growth Imperative

Over decades of owning my own business, I've seen the economy go through many cycles. Most recessions were tough but were followed by a period of sustained economic growth. But as we've learned in recent years, not every recovery is the same.

As a business owner or senior manager, you need to be prepared for any contingency in business. What can be done to reignite growth in a company, in employees, in customers, and eventually in the economy? How can senior management reignite their company to achieve growth during economic stagnation? How can business owners motivate, excite, and get their company moving forward when so much news about the economy is mediocre or worse?

The answer is to think *big*. Think beyond tomorrow. Think optimistically, and look for interesting and emerging bright spots in the economy.

Here are just a few recent disruptive events that have provided new opportunities for business:

Big data is revolutionizing marketing and sales. There are new ways to mine your own data and to reach your customers with more meaningful and cost-efficient one-on-one offerings. This is happening right now, and the potential growth outcome can be significant for most companies. Learning how to leverage big data to benefit your company should be a top priority for growth.

The cost of energy, which has been a heavy tax on our economy since the 1970s, is going down due to the growth of natural gas and recent major oil finds. America can hopefully expect to count on cheaper energy in the future, which will positively impact consumers and lower the cost of manufacturing in the US. How can your company grow by taking advantage of less expensive energy?

When you think about growth, it's important to remember that not all of it comes from the high tech sector. Consider the newest findings from Millward Brown's BrandZ "top risers" report, which indicates that Subway increased its brand value by 5,145 percent since 2006 and Apple increased its brand value by 1,045 percent. Both companies have built their brand by delivering a consistent, high-quality customer experience, which is a key to growth.

One of my favorite clients was a genius when it came to generating big ideas for growth. His name is Bob Reisner, and he ran a business unit of GE Capital. Bob would start a new brainstorming meeting by saying, "How would you approach this challenge if money were not an issue?" It was amazing how that one phrase opened up so many possibilities. Of course, money was *always* an issue, but what his statement did was to remove the constraining blinders for the purpose of generating new ideas and thinking big thoughts. He went on to spin off a business unit, which evolved into an Initial Public Offering (IPO). I was rewarded with a board position in his new company.

Growth is about finding the right opportunities and building a strategy to differentiate and build your business model.

How to Build a Powerful Brand

(This segment written cooperatively with Beth Flom, Director, Strategy, Tenet Partners)

There are Five Key Drivers to assure consistently strong brands. Using several brands that recently ranked in Tenet's CoreBrand® Top 100 Powerful Brands as examples, we've culled some specific tips for building (and maintaining) a powerful brand.

SPEND MORE – Great brands spend more aggressively on advertising. According to a recent report from Kantar Media, while advertising expenditures declined overall in 2013, spending among the ten largest advertisers for the first nine months of 2013 increased by 6.4 percent.

Though not a standalone strategy, advertising is a way to help increase a brand's power because it enables that brand to control the message and, therefore, communicate more distinctive, emotional benefits. While other companies may be able to mimic product or service attributes, the combination of an organization's culture, personality, and processes inform how those products and services are delivered. As the foundation of advertising messaging, this more emotionally driven approach helps create differentiation, favorability, and lock-in.

SAY LESS – After suggesting you spend more on advertising, simultaneously – suggesting that you say less may seem counterintuitive. We understand that increased advertising helps you speak in more places – in magazines, on billboards, and online. However, saying less enables you to focus on the pure essence of your message in those places. Hone your communications to just a few clear, simple, and believable statements. And repeat them consistently and frequently.

Strong brands have high familiarity, meaning stakeholders understand what a company does in totality. Consider PepsiCo as an example. PepsiCo was for a long time perceived as solely a beverage company. However, recent communications have made a concerted effort to communicate the company's better-for-you strategy that, in part, includes its very successful snacks division. Clearly, this powerful brand understands that familiarity must go beyond name recognition to achieve a more comprehensive understanding of the organization as a whole.

BUILD TRUST – Our most recent Top 100 Most Powerful Brands report notes that distrust in brands is declining, but trust has been slower to recover. This is especially true when it comes to trusting management, a key factor in building and maintaining the favorability necessary to become a powerful brand.

Nowhere is this trend more apparent than within the financial services sector. Financial services buyers indicate that what's most important to them are softer variables like trust, transparency, and accountability. In an industry crippled by controversy and distrust, there has been a keen understanding of this buyer tendency and a collective effort to rebuild the trust of consumers through communications. Perhaps, as a result, companies including Charles Schwab, JP Morgan Chase, Merrill Lynch, and American Express saw advances this year in terms of their brands' power.

PERFORM WELL – Here, we speak not only of your financial performance, an important component of the favorability required to being a powerful brand but also of your operational performance. Strong brands require follow-through and an internal process and culture that enables your employees to live the brand and deliver it consistently to your customers.

Amazon is one of the best brands, partly because the company understands performance. Always known for its superior customer service and for giving employees the freedom to make the right decisions for customers, Amazon has recently topped itself. Take, for example, the company's "Mayday" feature incorporated in its latest Kindles. With the press of one button, customers can access a real person – in real time with real answers. It doesn't get much more powerful than that.

BE TRANSPARENT – In the absence of a proactive message, customers create their own message based on experience or hearsay. In today's age of social and viral media, arming your customers as brand ambassadors has become alarmingly more important. Delivering consistent and pervasive messages is the first step. Taking responsibility and offering a track record of honesty increases trust and favorability and is but another means of building a powerful brand.

For instance, Unilever's Ben & Jerry's customers can easily find the following statement on its website: "Ben & Jerry's is proud to stand with the growing consumer movement for transparency and the right to know what's in our food supply by supporting mandatory GMO labeling legislation." Yet the company goes on to acknowledge that this is a process – they will not be able to source all non-GMO ingredients immediately but are committed to doing so over time. The ultimate result is that consumers feel understood and valued, and Ben & Jerry's has generated brand power through transparency.

As the midpoint between art and science, branding requires both creativity and practicality. Consider these key drivers as you build your powerful brand.

CHAPTER 5

Brand Accountability

Long-term strategic brand planning and building can significantly impact corporate financial performance. Such planning requires understanding the dynamics of the world economy as well as the industries in which your business competes. Brand planning also depends upon the depth of your connection with your most important constituents – those who create your brand's reputation.

Brand planning deepens connections and cohesion. When leaders fail to actively manage the corporate brand, we see a phenomenon called brand reputation drag. Logic and cohesion evaporate, the brand loses its resonance with internal audiences, and external audiences show confusion. This leads to financial underperformance and the erosion of reputation and value. Ultimately, the brand collapses. Remember – great brands demand great leaders, and weak or corrupt leaders can destroy great brands.

To avoid such a fate, you need a well-planned, well-executed corporate branding campaign *that clearly, concisely, and consistently communicates your corporate strategic direction.* Such a major and vital communication effort must be enthusiastically embraced at the highest levels of the company. Who decides that vision? Traditional thinking says the responsibility for the company's image resides with the chief executive officer.

Beyond the CEO

The CEO's principal role is to encourage and manage the long-term health of the entire enterprise, including its corporate brand. As we have already mentioned, everything a company says or does affects brand perception, and the CEO is the one person charged with managing company performance and with especially meeting financial goals. Accordingly, it is common for CEOs to believe that corporate brand strategy lies alone entirely in their realm of influence. However, a corporate brand should transcend a single CEO. It should be part of the DNA of a corporation, and, therefore, its health should be overseen by a higher and broader group responsible for the long-term health of the company – its board of directors.

Any successful brand must be nimble and dynamic. It must adapt to new needs and market realities. This means brand direction may change when market forces warrant it. Adapt or perish, swim or sink, move or die. Because the value of a corporate brand has an enormous impact on the market capitalization of a corporation, it demands the attention and oversight of the board of directors.

As advisors and overseers of the CEO, board members should monitor the long-term health of the corporate brand. They provide a robust check and balance by reminding senior executives to nurture this intangible asset with tangible value and by helping these executives understand how to manage it in order to maximize return and increase the overall corporate value. There is no more important role a board can play.

Consequently, giving the board of directors oversight of the corporate brand is crucial to the long-term health of your company.

Board Responsibility for the Corporate Brand

Long-term, strategic brand building can have a significant impact on the financial performance of a company. Understanding the dynamics of the economy, your industry, and your direct peer group via an ongoing, structured evaluation are critical to managing a corporate brand as an asset.

When a company does not actively manage its corporate brand, the logic and cohesion of the company's strategic direction loses resonance among management and employees. This creates "drag" on the company, which eventually leads to underperformance of the company's financial results, including its stock price.

Corporate branding communications campaigns are essential for most corporations, but especially for holding companies. These campaigns, which are so important to projecting the strategic direction, should be protected, and even funded, at the board of directors' level. Corporate brands are long-term investments with returns best measured over years, not by quarters.

Your corporate branding campaign is basically the communication of the strategic direction of the company. To manage this important intangible asset, the brand must be viewed somewhat differently than other company assets. Communicating the corporate brand is critical to a company's success and should supersede the sphere of traditional corporate hierarchy. Giving the board oversight for the corporate brand does not mean board members should climb into the trenches on the execution of corporate brand campaigns. Rather, they should be actively involved in understanding and managing the strategic intent of the long-term health of the corporate brand.

CEOs and Chief Marketing Officers (CMOs) might argue this infringes on their territory, but the impact of the corporate brand on market capitalization makes it an exception that deserves the attention and oversight of the board of directors.

The board's engagement also creates a healthy check and balance in brand management. For instance, some senior executives underestimate the tremendous value of this intangible asset. Others have difficulty understanding how to maximize the potential return, which can often be a significant driver of corporate value.

The board of directors can balance these missed opportunities. Boards should have oversight and ultimate responsibility for the long-term health, vitality, and value creation of the corporate brand. The board should expect a CEO to develop a plan to build and nurture the corporate brand and to report on its value on a quarterly basis.

Corporate Branding and Its Impact on Enterprise Value

We know from our extensive proprietary research that a direct relationship exists between the strength of the corporate brand and stock performance. *You will see more about this in the next chapter.*

Corporate brand equity value is a stable, predictable, and identifiable value that we believe should appear in the corporate annual report. At the very least, the value should be reported in the footnotes – similar to the way oil companies report known reserves or pharmaceutical companies report drugs in development. At this time, corporate brand equity value isn't part of the Generally Accepted Accounting Principles (GAAP) and, therefore, might be met with some resistance, despite representing significant corporate value.

The Brand is a Business Asset

Another argument for the board's responsibility for the brand is that most CEOs and Chief Financial Officers (CFOs) tend to underfund marketing programs. The problem is they tend to look at the corporate marketing budget as an expense and not as an investment. The missing ingredient has been reliable financial metrics that tie marketing performance to growth and ROI. This lack of standard financial metrics has created a chasm between CMOs and CEOs/ CFOs. Understanding the significant financial value related to the management of the corporate brand as well as having a systematic method to evaluate improvements in perception will result in an improved financial performance. Brand budgets, like any other investment, should be based upon potential value creation. Corporate branding is an investment, not an expense.

The brand is a business asset, which can – and should – be managed over time in the same manner as any other business asset. While no two companies are exactly alike, it is important to develop a standard set of metrics and reporting methods to determine the financial value of the company brand and identify specific strategies, including budget allocation, to increase a company's "brand power."

PRODUCT BRANDS DRIVE REVENUE. CORPORATE BRANDS DRIVE BUSINESS

CEOs and CFOs will no longer need to wonder where the investment in the brand is going. Brand investments will be held to the same standards of accountability as every other aspect of the business.

Consistent reporting of the corporate brand as an identifiable intangible asset to the board of directors makes it one of the most valuable assets a company possesses. It's a powerful engine that can drive a business forward.

Branding a company pays dividends. The results are dramatic and include measurable correlations between brand recognition, sales growth, and stock value for entire industries as well as for individual companies.

CMOs, CEOs, CFOs, and the board of directors should have the ability and take responsibility to track investments in corporate communications to demonstrate success with ROI measures – the gold standard for corporate decisions.

RECOMMENDATIONS TO BUILD AND MANAGE BRAND VALUE

We promote the concept that corporate brands have value and should be managed like any other asset.

The board should "own" the corporate brand – retaining an oversight role.

The board should insist that the CEO measure and report on the value of the corporate brand on a quarterly basis.

The corporate brand should be continuously measured to identify any weaknesses in the corporate business strategy before it's too late to correct them.

Brand equity valuation will identify the significant value of the corporate brand. Understand that value to help determine if an investment in building the corporate brand is worth the expense.

Manage and compare your corporate brand to competitive companies as well as evaluate it against peers and industries.

The Brand and Stock Value

Whether it sells apples or Apples, products or ideas, a company is only as valuable as its brand is desirable. Apple is just another computer/phone company without its millions of brand loyalists. The "brand," you see, is more than simply the product for sale or the Under Armour logo on Jordan Spieth's golfing attire. The brand is your concept of that product or the service you sell. It is a reflection of the fundamental values of your people and your customers. It is how you see yourself, how you see your product, and how you see your customer.

Consider the immense power of a single commercial conceived by Ridley Scott of Chiat/Day for its client Apple when the company introduced the McIntosh. The ad ran only one time during the Super Bowl; it was called, "1984", and it not only changed the company but the world. The truly great have powerful, coherent visions of their brands that resonate with their publics because their visions are clearly and consistently communicated.

Tenet's extensive research has proven again and again that corporate brand performance (its strength) correlates directly with stock value (price and appeal). When a brand underperforms, its stock sinks. When it performs masterfully, its stocks rise. From the mountain of data we have accumulated over the past twenty-five years, we have developed and honed a precise methodology for analyzing brand value, targeting areas of weakness, and helping companies develop a clear, concise, and enduring brand vision that is relayed clearly, concisely, and consistently – the key to a superstar brand and, therefore, to a powerhouse company.

Because corporate brands correlate directly and consistently with stock value, I believe they should be recognized as a definable asset, just as any asset or liability from cash to debt, from real estate to inventory, from patents to R&D. For now, "brand equity" is excluded from Generally Accepted Accounting Principles (GAAP) and is rarely even a footnote in annual reports coming out of most CPA offices. Yet, accounting standards are rapidly changing around the globe. It should be incumbent upon senior leadership at every corporation to proactively assess, evaluate, and declare the value of their corporate brands before GAAP standards demand it. Waiting to do otherwise would be unwise. Why? Because eventually full disclosure will include brand valuation, and all investors will better understand the value of their investments and demand it.

We predict that corporate brand value will be added to financial reporting standards within the decade. That means investors, employees, managers, and especially board members need to be well-versed on brand valuation methodology and understand how data generated by those methods will impact the financial accountability of their investments in brand marketing. Understanding corporate brand valuation methodology means you will be prepared for changes in accounting rules and, more importantly, ready to maximize your corporation's overall value.

Tenet's model is called the CoreBrand Index® (CBI). It represents twenty-five years of development and delivering continuous quantitative research study and regression models to demonstrate the undeniable predictive influence that brand value exerts on corporate stock value. We evaluate brand value according to the strength of four areas:

#1 The familiarity and coherence of the brand

#2 The reputation of the company

#3 The respect external audiences extend to its leadership and brand ambassadors (employees)

#4 The investment potential financial audiences hold for purchasing decisions, including whether to invest in the company's stock

---

The quantitative research study began in the US in 1990. Today, more than one thousand companies across fifty industries are continuously researched and their brand values calculated so that they can create strategies to improve performance and, therefore, improve stock value, too. The vast tide of CBI data demonstrates that corporate brand has numerous vital financial valuation properties:

It represents future cash flow.

It is accurately and consistently measured.

It is accurately and consistently valued.

It can be compared to competitive companies and industries.

It can be managed like other assets — including budgeting.

It can grow or lose value over time.

It can be evaluated on an ROI basis.

It can be used as a company-wide management tool.

It provides a dashboard measure on corporate health.

The Brand as a Dashboard

These criteria are like the displays on your car dashboard. They provide a quick and reliable indicator of the health of your corporate engine – information vital to the financial advisors and shareholders who shape the company's future. Notably, these criteria are among those that the Financial Accounting Standards Board (FASB) consider necessary for inclusion as a financial standard in the Generally Accepted Accounting Principles (GAAP) of the International Accounting Standards Board (IASB).

Investors, employees, managers, and especially board members should study and understand how to evaluate brands and how the resultant data impacts corporate value. By understanding corporate brand valuation methodology, you will be better prepared to manage changes in accounting rules and ready to lead your company to brand brilliance.

CHAPTER 6

Corporate Brand Investment:
Enviable ROI

We have established that corporate brand strength (broken down into the elements of Familiarity, Coherence, Reputation, Leadership, and Investment Worthiness) is an indicator of future corporate cash flow. It is a valuable asset that can be accurately and consistently measured, valued, and compared with that of competitors. It can gain or lose value, and it can be evaluated on an ROI basis. And finally, it can be deployed, managed, and measured company-wide. This dashboard data provides senior executives, board members, and financial advisors with a snapshot of the health and vitality of your corporate engine – or, more specifically, what drives your "Corporate Capital" engine. So how do you create that dashboard?

Reliable Metrics – Simple and Easy to Compare

The first step toward understanding research data is to put your corporate brand in the context of its peers. Comparing your brand's value to that of others in your industry or core business offers a sound indicator of its overall health.

Let's look at the actions of a company that undertook a competitive analysis. Here, the company had a critical competitive advantage and wanted to expand it. Leadership allocated $24 million toward a sixteen-month communications campaign that used a wide variety of media to emphasize corporate brand strengths. In one year, CBI measures demonstrated that the client's brand equity increased by a whopping 2.1 percent of the corporation's total market capitalization, which is over the performance of peer companies during the campaign:

Brand Equity Competitor Analysis

	Q1	Q2	Q3	Q4	Q5	Q6
Peer Avg. Brand Equity (Percent)	6.8%	6.6%	6.4%	6.1%	5.5%	5.4%
Client Brand Equity (Percent)	8.1%	8.2%	8.4%	8.8%	8.9%	8.9%
Client Brand Equity Net Gain (Percent)	0.0%	0.3%	0.7%	1.4%	2.1%	2.2%
Communications Pressure ($mmm)	$0	$5	$8	$9	$2	$0
Cumulative Spending ($mmm)	$0	$5	$13	$22	$24	$0

Source: Tenet's CoreBrand® Index

The CMO needs reliable financial metrics like those in the chart above that link brand-building communications efforts to overall corporate growth. Without them, the CMOs have no way to measure the success of the investments. Such tools give them the data they need to make rational arguments to skeptical chief executive officers or wary chief financial officers.

Brand 4 Cs: Coherent, Clear, and Consistent Communications

Companies need a systematic method for evaluating improvements in brand familiarity, brand coherence, and brand reputation and a keen awareness of how strength or weakness in any of these characteristics is linked to executive leadership and its ability to promote a clear, concise, and enduring vision supported by clear, concise, and consistent brand-building campaigns.

By using our own CBI, all of this good work can be correlated to overall financial value performance – and thus shareholder value. It can be measured and proven. Investments in corporate brand-building communications campaigns then can be evaluated and adjusted to meet the need and achieve the desired ROI, whatever it may be.

The brand is a business asset, which can – and should – be managed over time in the same manner as any other business asset. While no two companies are exactly alike, it is important to develop a standard set of metrics and reporting methods to determine the financial value of the company brand and identify specific strategies, including budget allocation, to increase a company's "brand power."

> **MESSAGE IN A BOTTLE**
>
> Coca-Cola. The name resonates with billions. Coca-Cola enjoys the highest brand equity in Tenet's CoreBrand® Index (CBI), with nearly twenty-one percent of its market capitalization linked to corporate brand value. Companies that enjoy high brand power almost universally see a corresponding high percentage of brand equity to market capitalization. That means they have much to gain from determined, sophisticated management of their corporate brand. So while Coca-Cola, Apple, and others stand at the pinnacle of brand equity, even companies in industries where brand identity is not as valuable to key audiences can increase market value dramatically through sound brand valuation and management.

CHAPTER 7

The Benefit of Ongoing Research

While the CEO and Board of Directors provide high-level focus (the vision), they rely on their senior management to identify tactics to build and maintain brand value (strategy) and on employees to carry out those ideas. No matter how visionary the leaders or how dedicated the managers and employees, top-performing companies need qualitative and quantitative research to crystallize their ideas or spark a rethinking.

BUILDING GUIDEPOSTS

To improve brand value, you have to know how your constituencies perceive your brand already. A small miscalculation could lead to years of determined, dedicated efforts – in the wrong direction. Research shows what is working, indicates areas of trouble, and spotlights well-managed areas. It provides the crucial information that grounds successful strategies and tactical solutions. It informs the CEO and the board and provides senior management with a roadmap. It defines equity value. It points out valuable leverage points. It measures ROI. In short, research is the dashboard, and its results are the dials and digital meters.

Every company has unique characteristics and challenges. The more we know about a corporate brand – how it is perceived in the marketplace, whether there are gaps between perception and reality, whether the proper audiences are following the brand, the quality of the leadership at C and Board levels, etc. – the more likely the success of the brand strategy. Research may provide most valuable guideposts. Well-planned and executed research provides:

Perspective and feedback and consequently builds trust between you and your key constituents (every audience that is critical to your success as a corporation);

Translations of key constituents needs and wants;

Information that empowers you to design and develop effective communication tools to reach diverse audiences;

Identification of brand attributes and industry drivers that you can put to good purpose;

Monitoring, comparing, and contrasting of your brand with peers to identify strengths and weaknesses, capitalize on competitive disadvantages, and motivate key constituents.

PRECISION TUNING

The more complex the company, the more indispensable ongoing research is. Like a high-performance automobile, a highly complex corporation requires precision management and built-in diagnostics to ensure that the engine (brand equity) is never compromised and is always filled with gas (corporate capital).

An ongoing quantitative market research program provides executive and senior management insight into their brand's performance with its diverse (and often cross-purpose) key constituents. One *cannot know too much* about the needs and wants of constituents or the shifts in your competitive landscape. In fact, understanding constituent attributes (e.g. who they are, what they need/want, how they vary from segment to segment, day to day, month to month, year to year) is crucial when structuring research.

Here are a few things senior managers will take into account when planning an ongoing research (evaluation) model:

WHAT time range will ensure cohesive and consistent results?

WHO best represents both internal and external perspectives that will result in the most objective, useful data?

HOW much are you willing to invest in order to reach a sampling audience large enough to ensure valid and useful data?

WHERE can you find the widest perspective, taking into account your budget? The broader the research, the better perspective you have of your place in the competitive landscape.

Effective Research: What It Takes

Poorly planned and executed brand valuation research is a waste of time. You must have well-defined, strategically based, and focused research to gain insights that empower senior management to develop strategies that connect the brand with its audience and elicit the response you desire. Sound simple? It isn't. Crafting research takes skill and experience. Here we outline the best practices for an *ongoing quantitative market research program* and the best methods you can employ to put research results (data) to use to polish your brands to diamond-level shine.

Seek Non-Aligned Insight

To understand and plan for brilliance in your corporate brand, you need the perspective of non-aligned audiences. Not your competitors – they have an ax to grind. Not your employees – they are biased. Not your vendors or retailers – their opinions count but are often clouded by their own needs and wants. Not your senior managers or board members – all offer great perspective but not the kind of unaligned insight you need most to help you define your brand's strengths and disadvantages. Even customers who drive your revenue may not have clear insight into your corporate brand.

For our CoreBrand Index®, we utilize a non-aligned management audience within industry to gain the best insight. The "non-aligned" – without them, your research will be no more useful than talking to yourself and just as inconclusive. We call this audience the Business Decision Makers (BDM). It is made up of well-educated, high-income "Influentials." In a perfect world, your ongoing research program will check in with them on a scheduled basis so that you may achieve continuous benchmarking.

Here's why: Believe it or not, your brand benefits richly when it considers the opinions of people who don't care whether you succeed or not. Your brand is of no consequence to them. It's nothing personal. In fact, their neutrality is their great value. Through them, that "mirror on the wall" reveals the truth. They will not call yours the fairest if your brand is not.

BDMs are the focus of much of our research at Tenet. We have been engaging and measuring their opinions on the CoreBrand Index® for more than twenty-five years. Who are they? They include independent industry analysts, market analysts, and financial planners at large and small investment companies as well as those in private practice whose voices have national respect. They include every aspect of leadership and management of companies that focus on the kinds of goods and services that you make and sell. They are also savvy investors, often managing multiple portfolios in addition to their own – they represent the important retail segment of the investing public.

A BDM is a valuable counterweight to the perspective of aligned (biased) audiences such as employees, loyal buyers, shareholders, competitors, and competitors' loyal (aligned) customers. A BDM takes a steely view of your company and sees how your brand may improve over time, but he also knows how to tell the difference between real improvement and – to borrow a phrase – irrational exuberance. A BDM provides reliable and effective comparisons between your brand and its competitors.

> **DON'T DRINK THE (APPLE-FLAVORED) KOOL-AID**
>
> There are no buyers and users more rabid about their brand than Apple users. But if Apple's senior management listened only to what its loyalists had to say, the brand would suffer greatly. Brand user data is the ultimate Kool-Aid – it tastes good and goes down smooth, but if that's all you drink, it will surely rot your teeth. *Aligned* audiences can provide valuable knowledge and insight, but they will skew data and prejudice findings if not balanced by insights from *non-aligned* constituents. Taken alone, aligned perspectives can poison the research results and keep the brand mired in the status quo, perpetuating brand strategies and tactics based on self-adulation and complacency. Great brands do not drink their own Kool-Aid, Apple-flavored or otherwise. They seek outside viewpoints that balance such data and make it relevant. You will find these truth-tellers in the media, in financial advising firms, and among those advising government leaders at national, regional, and local levels. They are aware of you, so you should be aware of them.

Aligned Audience Viewpoints

Aligned Audience Viewpoints (AAVs) are subjective – but they afford indispensable insight into your brand's strengths and weaknesses. For any ongoing quantitative market research program to be of value to planning and tracking, senior management must demand that it include benchmark tracking across every level within the company, from leaders in the C-level offices and down through the ranks of senior and middle management.

Good research must track AAV behavior, performance, and opinion onto the factory floor, out to the dock and logistics managers, and back to the sales team. But remember, although far down the chain of command, employees dealing directly with customers offer some of the best insights. Field sales agents, deliverymen, customer service/call center agents, and retail sales staff all have timely, valuable information on brand strength and performance.

But don't stop there. Reach beyond the confines of the corporation to include other valuable AAV segments such as end-users/consumers, manufacturer suppliers, value-added resellers, most-admired peers, and feared competitors. Their responses should be displayed on the dials of your brand engine dashboard. They, too, have a story to tell that reveals much about what is right – or wrong – with your brand's strength (value) and performance.

Putting Data to Work

Data that is the result of robust brand research is as valuable as any raw material. It grows in value as it is refined from raw data into a high-grade fuel that can create change and growth within a company.

You need researchers with sharp analytic skills and patience to sort through the data. Data sorting means sifting through the many opinions from interviewees. For any of it to make sense, the opinions need to be categorized and prioritized then correlated within their categories and compared to those outside it. What the CFO thinks about the company's share price can be far different from what a financial analyst thinks about it. While the CFO's opinion may carry more weight inside the company, the outsider's view tempers it, revealing gaps between perception and reality.

When crafting value-based research models, make sure you ascertain the following:

Detect the difference between a strategic insight and a casual observation.

Deploy contradictory and complementary viewpoints to establish the contextual framework for ongoing brand valuation.

Define the scope of research (whom to interview) within parameters of schedule and budget.

Define the frequency (how often to interview) of research within parameters of schedule and budget.

Deploy scope and frequency as tools to sift through predictable data in search of those gold nuggets that can forecast perception problems before they become realities that drive down brand value.

CHAPTER 8

Achieving Coherence with Brand Communications

By now, you should be convinced that brand value contributes to corporate success. In keeping with the prominence of its role, the brand must be carefully crafted and meticulously maintained at the most senior levels of the enterprise through intelligent investment and enlightened management.

Another key thought to remember is that everything the company says and does, whether planned or unplanned, communicates and shapes brand experience. When you consciously manage the brand experience through business processes, culture, and communications, it builds and improves the corporate brand. That measure of the corporate brand is what we call Brand Power. Brand Power is the familiarity and favorability of key audiences toward the brand.

All key audiences see the brand through a series of lenses called touchpoints. There is an opportunity to manage the brand at every touchpoint. Every audience will achieve either a positive or a negative relationship with the brand at each touchpoint. We call this "The Brand Experience."

The first lens is the business process or the practices making the company function. These are usually universal practices consistent throughout the organization that can indicate such information as how it makes money and how it performs as a business entity.

The second lens is a combination of culture and behavior. The culture of an organization can either destroy or build a brand. Think of Apple's culture and how it impacts every aspect of the brand experience. Every action becomes a brand event. As an example

I was recently standing outside an Apple Store just before opening – as the store opened all the employees applauded the customers waiting to enter. Apple is a great example of how to think about the culture and behavior that builds a total brand experience.

And finally, there is the communications lens. The broadest sense of the presentation is communications, both planned and unplanned. Communications includes your logo, signage, and advertising. It also includes how the receptionist answers the telephone or even a senior manangement's inappropriate remark caught on an open microphone. Everything matters. Taken together, the brand experience is seen through these lenses of business processes, culture, and communications.

The following chapter, divided into nine steps, addresses well-planned communications that can have a positive impact on your brand value and your brand experience.

Nine Steps to Effective Brand Communication

STEP ONE – BRAND STRATEGY

Distinguishing Your Brand in the Marketplace

The first step in this process is to make sure your brand strategy is in place. Brand strategy necessarily follows the company's business strategy. Is the company's business strategy clear? Does the senior management team understand the business strategy? If so, you can then build a brand strategy designed to help the business strategy meet its goals. The best brand strategies are designed with a clear purpose, are built to stand the test of time, and are flexible enough to adjust should the business strategy be required to change.

Identifying the key audiences of your brand strategy is absolutely critical to your growth and survival. How well do you know and understand those audiences? Some typical key audiences are employees, customers, business leaders, media, stockholders, the financial community, regulators, and competitors. If you are not doing ongoing benchmark tracking of the audiences critical to your growth and survival, then you are probably not going to be able to grow your brand in a meaningful and measurable manner.

Whether you are a nonprofit or a for-profit organization, one of the most important things to do is to identify your key audiences. The next step is to put them in an order of importance and then measure those audiences consistently over time.

STEP TWO – THE BRAND AUDIT

The State of the Brand Today

Customer research can give insight into buying decisions at any level of your distribution network, from wholesaler/distributor/reseller to retail sales outlets. But will that information let you see what your customers see when they come across your brand in the marketplace? We think not.

For a comprehensive view, consider a brand audit. These relatively low-tech, labor-intensive presentations are often organized inside a "war room" setting that lets you see all your communication elements simultaneously. The brand audit should delineate and describe any media used to convey visual, spoken, or written messages and show how those messages appear in current packaging, vehicles, uniforms, and signage as well as in TV/print/web advertising. That visual audit must include peer-level competitors to allow you to see the brand in the context of others. The audit will reveal strengths and weaknesses, assets and liabilities, advantages, and vulnerabilities.

Chances are no one in your organization has ever looked at all these elements side by side – or if they have, they haven't done so in years. Many C-suite executives and senior managers are often stunned at the level of disarray, redundancy, and inconsistency revealed in visual audits. Thankfully, every challenge is also an opportunity to improve your brand's strength. Knowledge is power.

An exhaustive audit will include any published matter that bears the company name, mark, and/or taglines, including online invoices, proposal covers, letterhead, sales collateral, direct mail, point of purchase displays, and sponsorship materials. Also included are printed or digital newsletters, product guides, promotional materials, and trade show graphics. Nothing is too picayune and nothing too large. MetLife shows up on a blimp. Intel appears on a microchip. Both influence how the brands are perceived, for better or worse.

STEP THREE – BRAND ARCHITECTURE

Strong Communication Foundation and Framework

Brand architecture provides the blueprint for brilliant brands and is the guiding principle for all forms of communication. It defines the brand foundation and the brand framework, making it the most essential component of effective brand communication. Whenever there is complexity due to acquisition, brand extension, brand proliferation, brand divestment, or other business factors, brand architecture provides the reference point so that executives can streamline and rationalize what brand characteristics to emphasize and which to let go. Consequently, the more brands you have in your portfolio, the stronger your brand architecture must be. The blueprint allows you to distinguish one brand from another within your portfolio and among competitors.

A brand audit will reveal the strengths and weaknesses of your brand architecture. Common weaknesses include inconsistent visual presentation, poor product differentiation, ill-timed product releases, muddled brand positioning, inaccurate audience targets, conflicting or unclear messaging, and inadequate research. All of these, if not managed, will eventually erode brand loyalty, decrease sales, and drive down market share and share value.

STEP FOUR – BRAND POSITIONING

How Your Brand Compares

To design an effective brand strategy, you must know how your brand is positioned among its competitors. To stand out, you must stand for something. The same is true for a brand. The vast wall of white space in a crowded market is an unforgiving backdrop.

Throw in competitors with very refined brand architecture, positioning, and platforms, and anyone can see that your brand must be distinguished in order to register with customers. It is not enough to simply stamp "different" on the soapbox. You must *define* that difference and integrate that message into every aspect of your communication. Then your brand's position within its competitive environment will be diamond clear.

STEP FIVE – BRAND PLATFORM

Promise, Personality, and Messaging

The next step is to articulate a defining brand platform. The brand platform gives life to the positioning. The brand platform is the core idea that unifies and motivates the organization. Up to this point, I've been talking about a concept. But now, we need to give it dimension and personality. These are the human attributes that define who we are and how we behave.

A brand platform, plain and simple, is what your brand stands for. It's the idea at the heart of your corporation, and it must be articulated with a clear and consistent brand communication program that adheres to the maxim "one brand, one voice." It defines what your brand is today and what it is likely to be in the future. Employee behavior and all business processes can be measured against it. The brand platform is composed of three parts: brand promise, brand personality, and brand messages.

Brand promise is the frank articulation of what the brand stands for at a fundamental level. Company XYZ has this brand promise, "Our products are made with the individual in mind. To prove that, they must set the industry standard for ease of use, portability, style, and cross-functionality. People who use our product get more out of life."

Brand personality paints the brand in human terms. For example, "Our products are fast, fun, and easy to use – they are extensions of the users, their sidekick or friend, their officemate or personal secretary. They are the loyal companions who can always be depended upon."

Brand messages are the key fact-based statements that support the less tangible claims of the promise and the personality.

- "Our products are ergonomic and easy to carry with you."
- "Our products are intuitive and easy to comprehend."
- "Our products may be customized to suit your personal needs."
- "Our products set industry standards in speed, power, and environmental responsibility."

STEP SIX – NAMES AND NAMING SYSTEMS

The Value of a Good Name

Many years ago, The New York Times took readers on a behind-the-scene look at the American Can Corporation's renaming as Primerica. In the story, the question was asked, "What do you call your baby if your baby is a bank?" The answer is not "The First National Bank of Bobby." Naming should never be personal. A name should be positioned to become the paramount written or verbal representation of brand that includes its values, its strengths, and its relationship to internal and external audiences. That takes determination, dedication, and a lot of time and money.

The name, logotype, mark, and symbol are highly visible elements of any brand. The naming process is detailed and attempts to maximize objective decision-making. Hundreds and hundreds of options will be created, measured against approved criteria, and then tested against consumer preferences until finally sent to lawyers for copyright and trademark research. Criteria may include such factors as executive preferences for coined names over descriptive names, attribute-based names over functionality-based names, any international restrictions, and concerns right down to the number of words, syllables, and characters used.

All great names have one thing in common: they satisfy the criteria and allow the new name to grow in value and meaning over time. They do not get in the way. They do not say or do too much. Time and consistent brand communication will accomplish that. Remember, *Coca-Cola*® was created as a name for a cocoa-infused, hand-mixed carbonated beverage created by a nineteenth-century pharmacist in Atlanta. More than a century later, it means so much more.

STEP SEVEN – IDENTITY

Logotypes, Marks, and Symbols

Identity encapsulates all elements that comprise a brand's foremost visual expression, including the name and logotype, mark, and/or symbol. This includes any graphic component of that identity such as color palette, proprietary fonts, colors, and the graphic hierarchy between its primary identifiers (e.g. Clorox®) and extensions (Clorox Soft Scrub®) or between the parent brand (The Ford Motor Company®) and its line brand (Ford Escape®).

An enduring identity is never trendy – it is an instant classic. It is the paramount visual representation of brand including its values, strengths, and relation to its internal and external audiences. The appropriateness and durability are the products of a design that is easy to apprehend and remember. Great corporate identities never leave the viewers shaking their heads in bafflement, even though they may leave something to their imaginations. Great corporate identities also reflect the company's certain place in history. To endure, they must evolve. They are never prisoners of a bygone era. In its long history, UPS updated its identity only four times but always retained the shield and the color brown.

STEP EIGHT – A UNIFIED VOICE

Consistent Content and Graphic Continuity

Where does your brand live? What elements convey its key messages? Upon which media is it broadcast? Across which marketing and communication disciplines is it developed, designed, and implemented? Who are its spokespersons, and who hears their voices and where? On the sales floor? On a sales call? Standing in a checkout line? Via direct mail or inbox-clogging e-blasts? In print, online, or via Twitter?

Brand communication is the sum of everything said, written, published, or conveyed that represents your brand. It blazes off the uniforms of employees and screams down from signs atop skyscrapers. Keeping that voice unified requires determination and discipline, but design success also requires giving leeway to your creative teams so that they can find new ways to talk about established brands that garner attention and drive market share. To that end, brand communication managers must encourage both conformity and nonconformity. How to do both?

Simple. Set standards and then challenge talented people to exercise unbridled creative thinking within those parameters. While this might sound impossible, it happens every day with great brands; brands such as Harrods®, Coke®, Dell®, Samsung®, Sony®, Virgin®, Honda®, Toyota® and Jack Daniels® did not grow by breaking the mold every day. They grew by respecting brand equity and finding ways to use it in new and exciting ways.

Whether it's a strategic branding assignment you need, a name for a new service, or a communication system for a new line of products, always look for partners who offer a combination of three critical ingredients: industry experience, marketing knowledge, and sheer creativity. Partners with those skills will surely meet your brand communication goals.

STEP NINE – BRAND GUIDELINES

Law and Order: Brand Guidelines Maintain Coherence

Sometimes it all comes down to organization. Senior managers and employees distributing communication or reviewing policy need to have these carefully crafted principles and parameters at their fingertips. Consequently, your company should create a "brand center" – an online site where all communications are indexed and saved both for reference and for compliance monitoring. Master files of all communication, including any corrections, are maintained here. And from here, those materials are reprinted or distributed through Content Management Systems (CMS) systems. The brand center serves as a single-source resource where anyone who engages the brand in internal or external communication can find guidelines and approved materials. The brand center also provides the resources for senior management to educate all employees about the brand architecture, strategy, platform, and positioning.

Brand centers must be custom-built. Here are some considerations that Tenet Partners takes into account when building compliance and control centers:

What kind of people will be managing the brand center? Brand experts? Marketing-communication experts? Low-level administrative support?

What kind of people will have access to the brand center? All internal employees? Some internal employees? External audiences, including clients, customers, and the media?

What kinds of resources will be made available? Which formats and platforms will users be accessing?

Will outside vendors such as web programmers, advertising creative teams, printers, graphic designers, writers, and other brand communication support types have access to your brand center?

What kinds of activities will users perform inside the brand center? Choose and download? Manipulate and edit files? Ask questions? Request files? Ask for technical support?

Brand guidelines and compliance tools allow your senior managers to maintain strategies that build brand strength and long-term shareholder value. Guidelines create consistency. Enforcement ensures compliance.

CHAPTER 9

Employee Engagement: Which Employees Build Brands Best?

(This chapter written cooperatively with Larry Oakner, Manager of Employee Engagement, Tenet Partners)

Years ago, as part of an employee engagement project for Caterpillar, the global equipment manufacturer, I toured their Belgian factory and came upon an engineer assembling a diesel engine the size of a large conference table.

Dressed in an immaculate shop coat and handling his tools with the skills of a dentist, the engineer walked me through various production strategies, and I asked him in my fractured French why he was taking such care to do his job. I knew he hadn't attended any of the brand training sessions I had been conducting. He set down his tools, wiped his hands, and then told me, "If this engine fails, the equipment goes down, which shuts down the contractor's job because he has to have the Caterpillar dealer's technician come out and fix it. So the contractor's business suffers, the dealer has to eat the cost of repair, and the reputation of Caterpillar has a mark against it. All because of me." That's true employee engagement.

The employees who can make or break a brand are often times the ones not facing customers. We call those employee-facing employees. While there may be several degrees of separation from their customer-facing colleagues, these internal workers are a critical part of your workforce.

They're the housekeepers who protect a hotel's brand by making sure your room is spotless. They're the material engineers who develop the polymers that make a product's colorful plastic containers. They're the actuaries who calculate an insurance premium. They're the assembly-line workers, the parts suppliers, the financial analysts, the underwriters, and the researchers – all the employees whose work contributes to their individual brands.

Many times, these employees are far down the chain from the actual client or customer. They may not get to see the end result of their labors, and so, they can be in danger of being disconnected from their brand. According to the 2013 Gallup State of the American Workplace survey, "employees in service or manufacturing… are least engaged" among all employee segments. Years of Gallup's statistics have proven that the more disengaged employees are, the greater the potential financial losses for the company.

All those non-customer facing employees really do have customers – their fellow employees. Organizations that recognize the importance of connecting the "back office" with the customer reap the rewards of greater engagement and productivity among their employees. When employees see how their individual jobs contribute to the big picture, it adds to their motivation to be engaged.

We helped the employees of one financial services firm make those connections. At an internal sales conference, we created an interactive exhibit for all employees – not just the sales people – to see how their work was an essential part of their investment products. Using photos and headline graphics, we captured stories that made the links for those employees who don't work directly with clients. One poster read, "I'm the technology and operations manager who developed the web solution to help manage the investments of Mary the teacher." To bring the point home, we even created "Mad Lib" type forms for exhibit visitors to fill out their own connection stories: I am the _____ who _____ for _____. And then, we shared their connection stories with the HR department to be used in training.

Another way to harness the power of a company's entire workforce is to make sure that all employees are engaged with the brand, and that includes the C-suite of chief executives. It's good practice for an organization to ensure that its leaders are as involved in brand management as everyone else. During one brand training session with a global vascular and cardiac surgery company, the CFO and the president of one of their divisions became passionately involved in a debate over who was the better brand advocate. The CFO won the argument, citing that his responsibility for the company's stock price – a highly emotional metric – made him a true brand master as "stocks and brands are emotional."

Whether from the top down or the bottom up, if the overall goal of employee engagement is to connect the workers with the organization to build a better brand, a powerful place to start is by connecting employees with each other.

Creating a Brand Driven Culture with your Employees

SIX IDEAS TO GET YOUR COMPANY "LIVING THE BRAND"

Your people are your brand. It's how they greet customers, answer their questions, prospect for business, and deliver your goods and services. In fact, research reveals that the majority of customers' perceptions about a company are determined by their experience with its employees. Even if your workers never go beyond the factory floor, you depend on all your employees to keep your company's promise to your customers.

To truly make your brand a part of your company's culture, you have to make it personal for your employees. That means translating your brand strategy into their everyday actions. It helps to work with all levels of an organization, starting with the CEO and the Board of Directors and including executive level vice-presidents, directors, and everyone vital to creating a brand impression – and that's *everyone* in the company.

It means creating "real life" brand definitions that are relevant and meaningful to all employees. Creating brand definitions is about explaining to employees why being brand-conscious matters. It helps them understand how putting thoughts into actions will create lasting brand impressions on customers or other key constituencies. It provides evidence of how business processes and the culture of the company communicate brand messages even if there isn't face-to-face contact with customers.

Branding on the Inside is Good for Business on the Outside

When employees better understand their brand, they're more likely to be engaged with their company and more productive at work. A Gallup survey proves the connection between internal employee engagement and profitability: disengaged employees cost an estimated $300 billion a year in lost productivity to the US economy. Studies like this demonstrate the value of your employees to your company's brand.

To make your brand more impactful, you need to inform, teach, and engage with your employees so they can understand and learn how to act "on-brand." Here are some simple guidelines that can help you go from informing employees about your brand goal to "Living the Brand."

KNOW YOUR INTERNAL AUDIENCE. Understand what your employees need to know, who influences them, and how they learn. Consider the different levels of knowledge, experience, and sophistication.

PUT A TEAM IN CHARGE. A multi-disciplinary team representing senior management, branding, HR, training, and internal communications will give you a broader perspective with more insight and guidance.

MAKE A COMMITMENT. An employee engagement program needs top-level buy-in and resources from senior leaders. You'll lose credibility if you start and stop halfway through a program.

COMMUNICATE EARLY AND OFTEN. Information is powerful. Timely, consistent responses to project deliverables will keep things moving. Don't let internal programs take second-place to business as usual.

EXPECT A LOUD RESPONSE. Channel the support of dedicated and engaged brand allies to lead those in the middle of the curve. Bring them along and ignore the vocal naysayers.

ENGAGE YOUR WHOLE COMPANY. Everyone must be involved. Branding is everyone's responsibility – from the top down and the bottom up.

Tenet's CoreBrand tracking studies reveal that companies that consistently rank at the top of Fortune's "Best Places to Work" pay close attention to their brands and the critical need for informing their employees. And the top ranked companies know that the more clarity they have about their brand with employees, the more it can lead to increased employee engagement. Assessing the employees' perspectives is critical to the process. The results help to create a more engaging brand that is both credible and compelling to all key audiences – and especially to employees.

When your employees are "Living the Brand," you'll observe a more intense sense of purpose throughout the company. You'll notice that your customers are easier to please, and customer satisfaction will be greater. You will also find that employee recruitment and retention costs are lower because everyone wants to work for a company with a purpose.

Frustrated When Employees Ignore Directives?

INITIATE THE "RULE OF SIX" FOR BETTER RESULTS

CEOs are often puzzled when a major new initiative has been announced but doesn't seem to gain traction within the company. As the CEO, you have prepared the strategy, developed all the plans carefully, and you know this is the right initiative for the company, but what was launched with what you thought was the appropriate solemnity seems to fall flat with employees.

Employees are not robots with an on/off switch. Announcements without enough internal marketing conviction from management are often greeted with skepticism or worse. Employees will resist changes perceived as inconsistent or inconvenient. Ignoring new management directives is sometimes seen as sport among employees at some companies, and resistance can spread faster than you can say "social media."

The **"Rule of Six"** is simply conveying your message in six different ways to convince your employees that the directive is real; it matters, and it will not go away if it is ignored.

The Rule of Six applies to both large and small companies. It can be executed internally through traditional speeches, newsletters, memos and internal blogs, and even through media advertising. The point is to treat the announcement like a strategic initiative and treat your employees like the critical audience they are and communicate with them accordingly.

One case study where the Rule of Six was successfully applied was after a contentious merger between two banks. When a new name was announced, the employees of both banks were very skeptical.

Over the weekend before the public announcement was made all new signage replaced the old name at every location, new collateral material was filtered throughout the system, and new business cards were placed on the desk of every employee along with a hat and corporate brochure with the new name. The Rule of Six campaign was then launched with announcements via webcast by the CEO to employees, a newspaper media campaign subliminally targeted the employees, and billboards were tactically located near every major branch or office. Was it a lot of work to accomplish and coordinate all the elements of the program? Yes, but employees realized there was no going back to the old name, and they began to act like one company.

In another case, a beloved CEO left a company unexpectedly. A new, highly competent CEO was hired, but employees decided to act out with some serious passive/aggressive behavior. When the CEO announced new initiatives, employees would nod their head in affirmation then consciously resist implementing the plans. The new CEO was perplexed and began to fire key management team members who couldn't keep their employees in line. An underground employee newsletter was established, and things quickly grew to a near revolt. The problem became a board issue. Had they chosen the wrong CEO? As a last ditch measure, a series of internal marketing campaigns were launched to take back the initiative from the troublemakers. A Rule of Six operation reaffirmed the vision and values of the company. The second wave focused on the goals of the business. The third wave focused on the importance of the excellent reputation the company maintained with its customers and within the communities. Each of these initiatives was communicated in six different ways so they would have significant impact and come across with overwhelming force – but not be seen as angry or vengeful. Within sixty days, the rebellion was over. Within a year, the CEO was winning great praise from the employees and the board.

When management announces a new initiative, you want the employees of your company to go through an acceptance process. It looks something like this:

INITIALLY, YOU WANT TO ESTABLISH "AWARENESS."

- **I KNOW...** Employees know that a brand initiative exists and can articulate the brand promise and mission.

THEN YOU WANT THEM TO "UNDERSTAND."

- **I KNOW WHY...** Employees can describe the ideal experience we intend to deliver to our customers and understand why it's important to the company's success.

NEXT, YOU WANT THEM TO BE FULLY "ENGAGED."

- **I BELIEVE**... Employees feel an emotional connection and believe they play a role in bringing the brand to life.

FINALLY, YOU WANT THEM TO TAKE A POSITIVE "ACTION."

- **I DELIVER**... Employees at all levels deliver consistently on the brand promise at all touchpoints and are enabled to do so by the organization.

Remember, if you're frustrated when key initiatives don't take hold at your company, simply apply the "Rule of Six" and you'll be amazed at the turnaround in attitude and understanding. It is a small price to pay for keeping your employees motivated and focused on those things that matter most in building your business.

CHAPTER 10

Building an Effective Brand Council

Brand Councils are an excellent tool for a time-strapped CEO to help manage, maintain, and maximize brands with authority.

Successful companies are nimble, fast moving, and continuously reinventing themselves to ensure maximum returns and to maintain relevance with their customers. New strategies are the hallmark of an ever-changing business landscape. There is good reason why corporations leverage brands to occupy some of the most valuable real estate in the world: a place in the consumer's brain.

Brand Councils, comprised of knowledge-based personnel, are designed to oversee the implementation of a strategically focused, integrated communications system across all touchpoints within an organization and with its customers.

The most successful branding programs reflect the vision and management of the CEO, but few CEOs have the time to closely oversee implementation. That responsibility falls to the Chief Marketing Officer (CMO). There are times, however, when periodic oversight by the CEO is not only needed to assure an alignment of brand with the vision but also to provide traction and accountability for the campaign where support is less than assured.

The Brand Council provides a diverse group of corporate thinkers a forum to conceive, discuss, explore, debate, and plan their business strategies in the most conducive atmosphere possible. Within their framework, Brand Councils can express diverse opinions and perspectives that will generate more effective solutions.

Ideally, either the CEO or the CMO should chair all Brand Council meetings because one of the two is needed to assign responsibility to other members of the council to conduct various parts of each meeting. Here is an organization example of a successful brand council at a large global company:

#1 EXECUTIVE BRAND COUNCIL – CEO, CMO, CFO, CRO (Chief Revenue Officer), Investor Relations, Human Resources, and Business Unit Heads (annual meeting or meet as necessary)

The Executive Brand Council is made up of senior officers. Its main role is to restate the message that the brand is the responsibility of the entire organization. When the CEO has a clear and consistent commitment to the brand, that commitment will flow through the various echelons of the corporation as a unified entity. The Executive Brand Council's primary purpose is to set budgets and approve overall brand strategy and direction.

#2 COMMUNICATIONS BRAND COUNCIL – a provider of global communications and marketing leadership (quarterly meetings)

This body implements the communications programs. The Communications Brand Council has to formulate, coordinate and execute the marketing and communications strategy based on the Executive Brand Council's approved budget and direction. Its meetings are designed to hold the communicators accountable for making sure that goals are met and to identify problems before they happen.

#3 PRESIDENT'S BRAND COUNCIL – an appointed cross-functional team of business managers (appointed by business unit presidents) to represent the business unit and their branding needs (annual meetings)

The President's Brand Council consists of multiple disciplines, including purchasing, graphics, marketing, sales, legal, accounting, procurement, production, administration, training, human resources, and public relations — key managers who control all brand touchpoints. The role of the President's Brand Council members is to identify the various requirements of the brand and to evangelize/proselytize the brand back to the various groups they represent.

Outside Consultants on the Brand Council

Ultimately, Brand Councils are designed to oversee the implementation of a more sophisticated and reliable integrated communications system across all touchpoints within an organization and outwardly to all customer groups. Sometimes a company won't have certain specialists on staff and will seek outside consultants to fill the role.

Two of the best brand councils I've served on was with Robert Zito when he was the Chief Marketing and Communications Officer at the New York Stock Exchange and later when he held the same position at Bristol-Myers Squibb. Bob included both staff members from the company and outside consultants who acted as full participants on each council, thus enriching the discussions and adding credibility to the councils themselves.

Another specialist to consider is a lobbyist or a knowledgeable Washington "beltway" insider. These types of people can be helpful by providing a government perspective on key regulatory issues.

There's no doubt the impact of social media and new technologies on products. These forces are extremely important to monitor over time as companies grow and diversify. Both an independent outside IT expert as well as a social media specialist might have a role on the council.

Facilitation of meetings is also something to consider for especially sensitive topics (e.g. internal politics, or management disputes). Sometimes it's easier for an outside consultant to make a point or get a task completed rather than an employee of the company.

Brand Councils Work for Every Company

At this point, you should not be thinking this internal organization is just for big companies. Brand Councils are great ways to get your team together and to make sure its members are all on the same page, no matter company's size. If I only had three people in my company, I'd still recommend having a brand council. It's a formal time set aside to discuss your brand strategy without the daily pressures that force tactical decisions rather than long-term strategy development.

CHAPTER 11

Customer Experience as a Value Driver

(This chapter written cooperatively with Hampton Bridwell, Chief Executive Officer, Tenet Partners)

The purpose of building a corporate or product brand is to gain and sustain a competitive advantage in your market. This comes from connecting activities together in such a way that they can't easily be replicated. If the brand is supported by activities that align with the business strategy, it will achieve differentiation and consistently better returns on your investment most of the time. Southwest Airlines has beaten every competitor in its industry for more than twenty years. They do it with a simple brand promise 'Dedication to the highest quality of Customer Service delivered with a sense of warmth, friendliness, individual pride, and Company Spirit'.

The very best brand strategy can be derailed instantly if customers have a bad interaction with the product or the service supporting it. The opportunity for failure is astronomical when you consider the myriad of things that can go wrong in any aspect of branding called "Customer Experience."

One way to evaluate the strength of your customer experience program is to try being a customer of your own brand. The actual purchase decision is often described as "the Moment of Truth" for your brand. Does every interaction build purposefully toward making the purchase of your product or service seemingly effortless and pleasurable? What about service after the sale? Does your brand deliver on its promise? Honestly, would you become a repeat customer of your own brand?

Creating and managing an exceptional customer experience for your target consumer is more akin to preparing to take them on "a journey of trust" with the journey's roadmap planned well in advance. The journey of the customer experience begins with your basic value proposition. As the customer's journey progresses, there are many interactions with the brand along the entire route. Consider what happens from the time the first advertisement is seen, to the website visit, to comparison-shopping, to the sales person, to the sale itself, and, of course, to interaction with the purchased product. Quantifying these experiences and analyzing the data will tell you if there are hidden potholes, detours, or anxiety causing bumps that damage your brand along the journey.

The corporate brand is a helpful tool for guiding the customer experience. Think of it as a radio beacon continuously emanating out of the corporate headquarters. Your beacon is radiating a signal like a radio station. The signal can be loud and clear, or it can be filled with static, depending on many different considerations – the power of the signal, distance from the station, atmospheric condition, etc. The radio station reaches varied audiences, including your customers, employees, investors, media, community leaders, etc. The signal of your corporate brand is broadcasting to all of these audiences and is transmitted through your business processes, the culture and behavior of employees, and all communications – whether planned or unplanned. At each of these intersections, or what we call "customer experience trust points," the signal has an opportunity to become distorted. Monitoring and tuning the signal to stay consistent is called "Managing the Customer Experience."

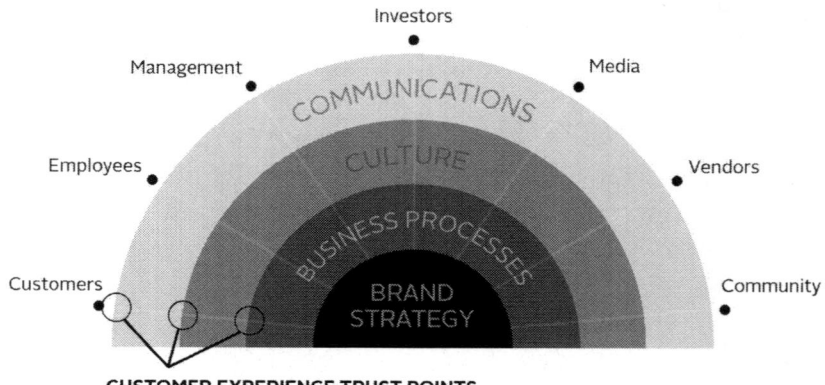

CUSTOMER EXPERIENCE TRUST POINTS

Managing the Customer Experience

The corporate brand is the signal emanating from the company. The signal crosses through the business processes, culture, and communications before reaching various critical audiences. Each of these interactions is a Customer Experience Trust Point.

The cruise line industry provides a vivid example of the potential for misalignment of the customer trust points between the brand strategy and the delivery of the service. The promise of the cruise industry's "business strategy" is for a fun, carefree, and relaxing voyage to exciting and exotic destinations. The "business processes" include strict safety rules for the sailing of the ships, food service, and cleanliness. The "culture" is how well the employees on the ship are trained to adhere to the safety rules while still maintaining an atmosphere conducive to the business strategy. "Communications" is everything from the advertising that captured the customer's attention and encouraged him to sign up for a particular cruise, to the passenger's boarding of the ship, to the announcement of bad news indicating a problem on the ship and how it will be handled, to disembarkation. Communicating in both good times and bad can help overcome problems and maintain customer loyalty even when a problem occurs.

Customer experience extends well beyond your customers. Other key audiences are diverse and influential such as employees, investors, media, etc. When building a brand, it's important to keep all key audiences in mind as if they are customers with the goal of understanding how each audience will respond to your brand message. Aligning thought and action from your brand to each audience is the essence of managing customer experiences to drive value.

Delivering on the Customer Experience

So who is ultimately responsible for delivering on the customer experience? The latest trends indicate the responsibility rests squarely on the shoulders of the CMO.

Tenet Partners conducted research with results showing that brands with high familiarity and favorability, combined with a rich customer experience, can have a premium brand value more than forty percent higher than their competitors. We know that consumers are more likely to trust, respect, and recommend these brands, creating a virtuous cycle for customers and shareholders. Customer experience, then, is an increasingly important point of delineation. Yet many companies still fail to deliver the experiences their customers expect. Why?

In Tenet Partners' consumer experience study, fifty-six percent of customers cited a poor service experience as the reason they left a brand. What would you do if half the customers abandoning your brand did so because someone on the front lines delivered a bad experience? I imagine that most CMOs would say that they would do whatever it takes to treat their customers better.

The problem is that the CMO has not traditionally been responsible for designing, delivering, and managing the customer experience. This is changing rapidly thanks to digital platforms that are remaking marketing, communications, and the delivery of customer experiences. CMOs at leading brands and forward-thinking companies are being asked to step into new operational areas to help craft and deliver the customer experience. In large part, the digital transformation of business models – and the resulting integration of brands into digital and physical touchpoints – is enabling and accelerating this shift in role.

Yet few executives stepping up to this new business challenge are truly prepared to tackle this domain because marketing has often in the past been isolated from operations. Traditional marketing has focused expressly on advertising and communications rather than on the overall experience. Fortunately, driving customer experience in a digitally-charged world leverages capabilities marketers already possess – specifically, the ability to gather market insights and develop brands that reposition companies toward market opportunity. However, in today's business world, more skills are needed to successfully address the bigger picture.

Marketers need to become engaged in and adept at developing business strategy, driving innovation, and implementing systems that shape the actions of entire organizations. These three dimensions, combined with a strong understanding of the brand, are the tools for driving growth. By engaging with their peers in the design of the business and digital platforms, CMOs help align the business model, culture, and operations to the brand, and companies with these skilled CMOs have a unique opportunity to deliver compelling customer experiences and create enormous competitive advantage.

American Express is one of the strongest brands, according to the thirty years of historical data contained within Tenet's CoreBrand Index®. It also scored well in our customer experience study. The story, especially versus Capital One, is very compelling. The research results show Amex users have higher levels of trust among customers, which is an essential element of brand loyalty. At a tactical level, the research also suggests that Amex, to a greater degree than Capital One, provides the knowledgeable help its customers expect. In addition, Amex engages with customers in a way that respects their unique needs. This incorporates orchestrating touchpoints across all channels, including digital. All of these activities are essential to providing a satisfactory experience.

A closer look reveals the impact of other innovations that Amex is employing for its platform. From everyday membership benefits to shaping mobile payment systems and driving fresh innovations to new markets, the company is steadily creating deeper levels of customer engagement. This, in turn, raises barriers to competing firms.

Bottom line: American Express focuses on the value it delivers through a highly tailored customer experience that is tightly aligned to its brand attributes. When compared to Capital One, which focuses its primary investment on growing its credit card share through advertising, American Express is winning the battle for the best, most loyal customers.

The lesson is clear. The tried and true pillars of service, value, and quality that are aligned with your brand and business model are still the most important. When CMOs concern themselves with value creation by delivering and managing a rich customer experience, they are not only driving marketing, they are driving competitive advantage and enterprise value.

When Does a Brand Lose its DNA?

We have loved JetBlue since the beginning of time, JetBlue's time that is. The concept of founder David Neeleman was simple and ingenious: he was offering not only a low-cost airline but also a pleasant customer experience. JetBlue managed and nurtured the customer's experience from the first website visit, to the purchase of tickets, to the arrival at the final destination. It was brilliant, differentiating, and successful, and it earned the airline a "most admired" status. As a customer, you felt that JetBlue was a different and very special company.

Mr. Neeleman not only often flew on the flights to actually experience "the customer experience", but he even served beverages and snacks to the travelers in order to empathize what it was like on the front lines of creating that customer experience. He talked with all of the customers who wanted to talk – every single one on the flight because he wanted to make sure he understood and lived the experience. Pleasing the customer was paramount.

The idea of giving reasonable legroom to customers was more important than losing a row of revenue. Putting video monitors at each seat to allow the live streaming of thirty-six television channels was breakthrough. If a monitor didn't work, and you couldn't get another seat, then you would automatically receive a refund for a portion of your trip. It was unbelievable customer service.

JetBlue was an airline that understood the customer experience, and it earned brand loyalty. The "True Blue" rewards program was a relatively quick way to get free tickets for loyal customers; it was a simple and easy way to get miles and to cash them in. Everything operated through the company's website, which was and still is intuitive and easy to use.

Not only did Mr. Neeleman put customers first, he also put employees at the top of the pyramid – one of the first airlines to do so. In 2002, he put his entire salary and bonus into the JetBlue Crewmember Crisis Fund, which was established for employees who had fallen on financial hardship. Employees loved, respected, and wanted to work for him.

Unfortunately, when an epic ice storm stranded JetBlue passengers on a runway on Valentine's Day in 2007, the tremendous goodwill toward the airline seemed to evaporate. Certainly, there were operational deficiencies at JetBlue, and Mr. Neeleman's explanation to the media that he was "mortified" didn't help. I believe the board of directors' decision to oust Neeleman as CEO was a bit of an overreaction. However, there were, evidently, other issues under the surface that nagged the board. In any event, with new management in place, changes started to come to JetBlue. It was slow at first, but the pace of change picked up, and like a jet reaching takeoff speed, the acceleration is continuing.

Under the new management, prices started inching up at a steady pace. JetBlue was known for very competitive fare, but that was changing, and prices went from inexpensive to downright steep. In the past, if a customer wanted to make changes to an itinerary, it would carry only minimal charges. After all, what does a change truly cost an airline when the customer does all the work online? Now, however, changes to itineraries are becoming significantly more expensive at $135 each. Exit rows were long desired by the taller passengers, so the airline decided to charge more for the "extra legroom seats." While just slightly more expensive at $10 in the beginning, they became much more expensive over time to $90 today for cross-country flights.

When many of the other airlines added baggage fees, JetBlue resisted. But rumors persisted that it would soon begin charging for checking bags, and now it is. Does this sound familiar? JetBlue is abandoning its founding DNA and following the playbook of the rest of the industry.

Shareholders have been demanding revenue and cash flow improvements, which is fine, but these shouldn't be coming at the cost of the brand. These nickel and dime changes are having an impact on the atmosphere of the customer experience. The fun is fading on JetBlue, and it is in danger of becoming a generic airline. With each change in its business strategy, the brand is starting to mimic the rest of the field. Unfortunately, the JetBlue experience is growing tarnished and undifferentiated, and over time, risks to the franchise will rise.

If you are a careful observer of corporate brands, you can tell when a company's brand is going through a "brand inflection point." They begin to hype things that don't seem natural to the brand – JetBlue is currently promoting a concept called, "Flying it Forward," which feels a little more like a publicity stunt than a genuinely altruistic good deed.

The most painfully obvious sign of a negative inflection point is JetBlue's plan to add a first-class section to their seating. Its "Mosaic" customers, those who travel the most, are given the opportunity to board first; maybe management will put a little blue carpet by the gate for them to walk across as they board. This will destroy the last vestige of the original, simple, and brilliant brand concept of egalitarian seating. JetBlue is losing what got it to the party: its differentiated brand and unique voice.

And we have seen this story before. When companies lose their DNA and their ability to deliver value through a differentiated customer experience, it heralds an usually a slow and painful downward spiral. But this can be easily avoided by giving your brand a purpose, having a strong brand DNA, and most importantly, having the strength to say no. Saying no to choices that mimic the customer experience strategies of competitors to chase short-term opportunities will be your greatest contribution to your brand's health and longevity.

How do all of these changes affect the bottom-line performance? For now, JetBlue stock is holding up very well against its competition. The shareholders are likely pleased with the changes. If JetBlue's all-important on-time arrivals start slipping, however, it could be in serious trouble. Will it be able to survive when its brand mirrors its competitors and it is without loyal JetBlue customers? Not likely.

It is both amusing and noteworthy that prior to writing this chapter, Hampton Bridwell and I discovered we had both separately written blogs on the same day about how the JetBlue brand was losing its strategic brand differentiation. You know the brand is losing altitude when two brand-conscious executives write about the same problem happening at two different locations at the same time!

CHAPTER 12

When to Rethink the Brand

The first thing to remember is that a brand is much more than just a logo. It encompasses everything that contributes to the customer experience, including culture and how you deliver your product or service. Your brand strategy is an essential business tool. No matter how attached you are to your brand promise or your current campaigns, if it's not helping you achieve your strategic goals, it may be time to take a fresh look at the strategy behind them.

Refreshing Your Brand Strategy

Here are five signs that it's time to reevaluate your brand strategy.

#1 YOUR BRAND SCORES ARE SLIPPING.

Akin to servicing a car, you need to keep tabs on the functioning of your brand. If you regularly research your brand's relevance with key audiences and periodically fine-tune your messaging, you will achieve more miles out of the brand than if you drive it off the showroom floor and never get it serviced. At a minimum, annual brand health surveys with external and internal audiences can keep you from suffering any major brand breakdowns. At best, you can solicit feedback in real time from your customers, employees, and constituencies that will enable you to respond quickly and efficiently.

#2 THE BUSINESS STRATEGY CHANGES.

Brand strategy always follows business strategy. Perhaps the leadership team has decided that doubling revenues by acquisition is the goal for the next five years. Maybe an IPO is in the not-so-distant future, or the opportunity has arisen to enter a new international market. As a critical tool for rationalizing your portfolio and building market appeal, your brand needs to align with, support, and reflect your business strategy. It is the story that holds your business together, and it must be told clearly and consistently to have proper impact.

#3 COMPETITIVE PRESSURES HAVE INCREASED.

Whether there are new entrants in your industry or a groundbreaking technological advance, when the dynamics of your industry shift, you need to make sure you aren't being left behind. "Clear, relevant, believable, and distinct" is the mantra we use to keep us on track when developing a brand positioning. When market dynamics change, so can your ability to stand out from the crowd and be unique. If a "me too" provider pops up with a vociferous awareness campaign, you run the danger of becoming a referential brand: "Yeah, we're just like X only we've been around longer." You need to retool your messages to stand apart, even if it's as simple as being sure to include your years of expertise in your outreach.

#4 YOUR BRAND EXPRESSION LOOKS DATED.

Ideally, your original brand strategy was both cutting edge and sustainable. Sometimes, however, market tastes shift beneath you. Just look at all of the companies out there with the word "cyber" in their name, or, more recently, how many logos have all colorful, lowercase, sans serif fonts. Whether it's an elegant refinement of your current logo or whether you start completely from scratch, your brand expression needs to match in tone and matter your cultural personality. You can't credibly claim to be innovative if your logo is stuck in the 1980s.

#5 YOU WANT TO SIGNAL CHANGE.

Sometimes you just need an opportunity to tell a new story. This could arise from having new leadership, changing your business strategy, or the sizeably shifting of your core audiences. Perhaps you've merged with another firm and together have more to offer than the sum of your parts. A refreshed look and feel, a new tagline, and possibly even a new name may be what you need to attract attention, build awareness, and capture the market share you desire.

Whatever the reason is for reevaluating your brand, whenever possible, existing brand equity should be retained. Just as when you're building your brand, whatever strategic and tactical plan you take on should be fact-based and built to achieve specific goals. Change should never be made simply for change's sake.

When and Why Should a Company Rebrand?

In the previous section, we talked about revamping the brand strategy. In this section, we are more focused on the communication aspects of the brand. The brand strategy may not have changed, but the visual and verbal components are crying out for a new coat of paint.

It may seem like it was just yesterday that you launched your new logo, website, signage, and advertising campaign. But time has a way of marching on, and now your marketing research team is telling you that it might be time for updates. What should you do and how often should you rebrand your company?

Let's assume that just today you launched a brand new positioning and identity program. In that case, I suggest market research to specifically evaluate the brand position be conducted at three-year intervals. This timing will allow you to correct any small issues or inconsistencies found by the research, and the basic positioning can be good to go for another three years. The three-year interval is long enough to help you recognize when change is needed and short enough that you will remain current with your industry.

Some industries, like technology, have a quicker servicing cycle of around two years. Conversely, industries like the electric utilities can usually utilize a longer four-year cycle. We recommend the three-year cycle for most industries as a good rule of thumb for researching the strength of your current brand positioning.

We find that most major repositioning programs are on a ten-year cycle – (3 x 3-year cycles + 1 year for the repositioning). While this all sounds very clear-cut and routine, you still have to deal with budgets, management changes, the economy, etc. It is usually a lumpier process than I've described, but I have found that if you explain your plans in advance to senior management and the board, they tend to understand this simple model and will accept it with less gnashing of teeth over the budget.

How Should You Rebrand?

Rebranding is a delicate issue requiring a balance between respecting the heritage of a brand and positioning it for the future. Tenet Partners has been at the center of hundreds of rebranding campaigns. Our point of view on rebranding is straightforward. The first rule is "Do no harm!" If the existing brand has value, don't make changes for change's sake. Make modifications to fix a problem or to fine-tune the strategic positioning or for a myriad of other reasons, but make sure the reasons are verified by research and not due to emotional knee-jerk reactions to something of little strategic importance.

Remember that rebranding a company is also an expensive process. You should only do it to solve a critical issue or to create a positive image if the current one is becoming lackluster. Again, consistent quantitative benchmark tracking market research of your key constituencies will tell you if ground is being lost to your competitors. When that starts to happen, it's time to consider rebranding.

Respect the History and Heritage of the Corporate Brand.

Finding the new brand positioning often begins with understanding the equity of the existing brand. Quite often, the founders of the company had a vision of the future that was more farsighted and universal, one which easily stands the test of time. Learn from their vision before developing a new one.

Once a new brand positioning has been fully explored, there are a number of steps that need to be taken to bring the new brand to life:

Build an updated brand architecture

Refresh or recreate the corporate identity

Prepare a communications strategy and rollout calendar

Test concepts with key constituencies to make sure they buy into it

Launch the new brand like you really mean it

- Big initial push with fanfare with everything launched at one time for practical purposes
- Events that include significant visibility of top management
- Sustained and consistent communications program supporting the new rebranding for a full year

If you truly want to see your rebranding campaign take hold and thrive, make the senior management team accountable for supporting the program. Make it part of the job review, and you will most certainly generate greater enthusiasm and support.

No matter where you are today in the process, it's never too early to start thinking about the next rebranding. Measuring periodically will help you get the most ROI out of your brand for years to come.

CHAPTER 13

Social Responsibility, Social Media, and Social Listening

Social Listening

UNDERSTANDING THE EMOTIONAL LEVERS THAT DRIVE BRAND VALUE

Social media is a key component in today's marketing mix. By its very nature, the communication in social media is fast and fluid, providing a unique, real-time perspective for gauging brand performance. Unfortunately, most efforts to understand the economic impact of social media are narrow in scope and lack detailed financial insights.

Research often in social media the attempts to identify the total volume of commentary and then use keyword searches to determine if the sentiment is positive, negative, or neutral. This approach, while useful, is often flawed because there are many nuances, such as sarcasm, that keyword searches are not equipped to analyze appropriately. The positive, neutral, and negative outcomes also do not provide sufficiently rigorous assessment to be prescriptive. They are useful in that they inform us about the nature of the conversation, but they don't address the "why."

Social listening and understanding begins with "Social Media Monitoring Analytics." The term refers to the process by which Tenet Partners' CoreBrand Analytics team, working in partnership with our colleague, Todd Powers, PhD, measures and evaluates social media. The approach involves gathering the relevant conversations on social media about a brand and then coding the emotional content of the postings using both machine-based algorithms and human coders.

This kind of "social listening" method identifies emotional dimensions as well as the specific individual emotional reactions to a given brand. This allows a more in-depth study of the nature of the conversations about the brand and the potential impact those conversations can have on it. We are learning about brand-specific messages and how target audiences are receiving those messages. This approach allows for the understanding of the emotional levers that drive customers as they move through the cognitive and emotional steps involved in the purchase decision process. Norms can be established for the product purchase process and this, in turn, helps determine where and how a specific brand succeeds or fails relative to its key competitors. This feedback on both products and their respective categories helps to identify the levers that can be manipulated to optimize the purchase decision journey.

For example, Dr. Powers and the Advertising Research Foundation (ARF) recently examined emotional patterns in the purchase process for packaged goods, automobiles, and smartphones. Surprisingly, postings on social media about smartphones were dramatically different from those in the other two categories. Buyers of smartphones were much more likely to express negative emotions like sadness, disgust, and anger, both early on (in the *problem definition* phase) and at the conclusion (in the *post-purchase* phase). The researchers were able to track the source of these negative reactions to resistance to forced upgrades and an inability to operate the "newfangled" devices, respectively. And this, in turn, led to a series of recommendations about how to market the products and position the brands more effectively.

The business objective is to identify how communications and the emotional content of social media are influencing the brand and, ultimately, the impact they are having on the desired outcomes such as revenue by target audience or channel. The desired business outcome is to optimize those communications levers to enhance the brand and maximize its financial performance.

To get to the point of optimizing return on communications investment requires a full examination of the value of the brand along with quantitative research of key targets to identify the strength, direction, and position of the brand relative to its peers. These standard benchmarks create a kind of laboratory that allows communications professionals to test ideas through controlled experimentation that examine cause and effect. This high-level diagnostic, combined with the specific "why" and "what" to do about it, provides a unique tool for identifying brand strengths (and weaknesses) by using the "social listening" data to find and examine the most relevant conversations taking place among the public.

By combining social listening with the financial measures of brand performance, companies can track and, importantly, manage the communications investments being made, the nature of the conversation, and the impact on the brand. Basically, we can observe and react to what consumers are saying (by audience and attribute), how it is being received, and the financial impact it is having on the brand. For example, financial companies like banks and investment firms have long known that "trust" is an important emotional determinant of brand affinity in their category. But social listening analysis has documented that trust is not necessarily a driving factor in the *information gathering* and *competitive comparison* phases of the purchase process where cognitive assessments carry greater weight in defining buyers' short-list of competitors. It is in the final decision – the actual *brand choice* – that trust is paramount. Combining the financial and emotional performance data for a brand will inform communications strategies going forward.

Many companies are measuring social media results, brand attributes, and brand impact, but they are doing so in isolation. What makes our approach unique and so effective in the marketplace is that it ties social listening to a quantitative analysis of the brand and methodologies to identify brand valuation and the resulting financial impact it is having. Social listening is a tool, but it needs to link to the emotional drivers of brand which, in turn, need to tie into financial performance in order to fully capitalize on the promise of social media.

Quality Trumps Quantity in Social Media Engagement

(This segment written cooperatively with Charles Muir, Marketing Analyst, Tenet Partners)

Social media is a critical component of the brand. It has become a marketing power with huge significance and requires equal amounts of strategy and instinct to best manage, utilize, and leverage. I've found five primary ways to build and manage social media efforts to effectively reach out to clients and build relationships.

Five ways to engage in quality social media:

#1 CHOOSE STRATEGICALLY YOUR PLATFORMS TO EFFECTIVELY ENGAGE YOUR CLIENTS.

While the primary social media outlets (Facebook, Twitter, YouTube) are the price of entry options, there's a continuously growing amount of secondary social media outlets you can utilize. Just don't try to have a presence in all of them. Remember, you can be part of anything, just not part of everything. Focus more on which outlets align with your company's services, products, and marketing style.

#2 KEEP AN EYE ON COMPETITOR USAGE OF SOCIAL MEDIA.

Each industry and market has a different entry level that has to be met for social media to get above the white noise. Some industries are better suited for YouTube rather than Facebook, Twitter rather than Instagram, or Vine rather than Reddit.

Keep a pulse on where your competitors are using social media, but also keep a close eye on where your clients' interest in social media. Find where those two segments align and, focus your social media efforts this calibration before experimenting with secondary or tertiary social media services.

#3 **USE THE 3/1 RULE OF KNOWLEDGE CONTRIBUTION VS. PRODUCT PROMOTION WHEN POSTING.**

Social media is not meant to be a source of high profits for a company. It's meant as a platform you can utilize to engage with clients and consumers. With that in mind, for every three posts of knowledge contribution where you provide something insightful or useful, you can post one service or product promotion.

The three parts advice to one part promotion is an effective balance for engaging clients via social media. If you inundate them with "Buy our service/product" posts too often, you will lose your audience.

#4 **EVOLVE YOUR WEBSITE WHEN APPROPRIATE TO PREVENT AGING.**

Websites are a standard price of entry you need in your social media arsenal. You can't just create a website and leave it content static for the next ten years. One design with non-updated content quickly grows stagnant.

Clients seek regularly updated content on websites so content should be updated weekly or monthly, depending on how closely engaged you are with clients. Website design should be reviewed at least every two years to ensure that you're providing an effective and efficient layout for clients to engage with you online.

#5 **UTILIZE THIRD-PARTY EXPERTS WHEN APPROPRIATE.**

Depending on your company's size and its bandwidth capability to focus on social media, utilizing a third-party service or independent contractor to help manage your social media efforts makes sense.

Make sure that you have a media strategy that you want accomplished, and make sure whatever third party you work with is in agreement and capable of achieving the results you want.

For Established Social Media Platforms and Strategies

These three initiatives prove best to leverage more established social media programs and to manage long-term maintenance of these campaigns.

Three long-term initiatives you should keep in mind for social media:

#1 LOOK FOR GENERAL TRENDS IN VISITS TO YOUR WEBSITE.

It is in your best interests to review your website statistics on a quarterly or at least a bi-annual basis.

Review visitor numbers to determine what times have the highest viewing rates. Time your marketing releases accordingly to reach the most viewers efficiently. Identify trending search terms that viewers use to find your website. Make an effort to post fresh content in relation to search terms growing in popularity.

#2 TRACE SOCIAL MEDIA CONTACT BACK TO YOUR MARKETING ACTIVITIES.

Keep track of who is following you on which social media platform. When clients/consumers reach out to you, make sure you can cross-reference them to determine how they found you or what marketing effort reached them. This is great for your marketing and sales teams to justify their various efforts.

#3 USE SOCIAL MEDIA SURVEYS TO GENERATE INSIGHTS INTO YOUR MARKETING.

It's worth utilizing a survey every year to generate insights into your marketing efforts. Reach out to clients who follow you on a social media outlet, and request their opinion on your company's services/products/marketing efforts. Entering participants into a raffle for a gift card or discount for your products/services provides an added incentive for participants.

Use the insights and answers compiled from the surveys to better leverage your marketing and sales initiatives.

Since social media by definition is more social than business, it's not as easy to quantify and qualify your efforts and engagements with clients. However, it's still worth the effort to strategically use social media to build relationships and engage with present and potentially future customers.

Corporate Social Responsibility for Every Company

Corporate Social Responsibility (CSR) is often confused with other terms such as sustainability, good corporate citizenship, ethical business practices, environmental responsibility, philanthropy, charitable giving, etc. While each of these is a form of CSR, when viewed collectively, they are an effective set of tools available to convey a leadership mindset focused on managing their corporation a part of the larger social fabric.

Even the term itself, "Corporate Social Responsibility", sounds like such a nuisance, and those who are busy running a small business may prefer to avoid it. However, when CSR is woven into your corporate DNA, you will find it one of the best ways to build your corporate brand and customer loyalty.

An excellent article entitled "The Path to Best in Class CSR: Deloitte", published in *Business & Leadership* (1/10/2014) by Brendan Jennings, managing partner, Deloitte, captures the essence of the issue. "What I don't want is for our staff to hear CSR and just think of volunteering, or something relating to the environment. Those things are all very important, and our people want to do them, but CSR is a much broader concept than that."

For Jennings, Deloitte's CSR positioning is a key component of its business strategy. "Organizations that are clear in their purpose achieve more. Our purpose is to be a quality provider of services… one that does its best for its clients, its people and the wider community, and one that can stand over everything it does."

Jennings goes on to say, "In relation to the clients we serve, it means doing our very best, for a fair fee. When it comes to our people, who are our greatest and indeed, only asset, if they believe in doing things the right way, good corporate governance is easier to ensure."

To identify the kind of CSR project that brings measurable ROI to a corporation, one needs to give it the same kind of thought that goes into building a marketing plan or a media strategy and be certain that it fits within the larger business strategy. Think about the essence of your company? What does it stand for? What do you believe in? Do some CSR programs resonate better than others? Is there one that clearly fits your business model? If you are lucky enough to find the perfect CSR fit, then you need to develop a plan to create differentiated positioning because the key to skillfully branding your company is differentiation!

Consistency, commitment, and communication are also important tools for redeeming the most valuable returns from the effort you make in CSR. I worked with The Reader's Digest Association prior to their initial public offering (IPO) and reviewed their many and generous CSR activities. One example is they provided funding for the massive beautiful vase of fresh flowers at the entrance of the Metropolitan Museum of Art in New York, but they never attached their name to the action. I pointed out that while an anonymous gift is admirable, it is also somewhat selfish. In my opinion, even a small, unobtrusive plaque is generating good will among key audiences such as RDA's employees who would also like to share in the good feeling achieved by a company's CSR program.

CSR checklist to remember:

Consumers are increasingly aware of sustainable business practices.

Consistent CSR practices lead to customer loyalty.

Employees care about your CSR programs and want to be involved if practical and aligned with their attitudes and beliefs.

Including CSR activities as part of your recruitment package will help to attract the most desirable and involved candidates.

If possible, you should own (brand) your signature CSR activity.

Know your suppliers and actively review their CSR policies to avoid risk to your brand (issues that could reflect poorly on your company).

As part of quantitative benchmark tracking reports, monitor social media to understand how your company's CSR policies are seen by others, and apprise monthly these findings to the CMO and CEO.

Train your management and employees with speaking skills that will enhance your CSR programs and ultimately maximize the recognition and goodwill created by these activities.

Deloitte's strategy was summed up: "It's a virtuous circle because good corporate governance, in turn, protects the business. 'When your people know why they are doing what they do, that helps protect not just the organization but the brand and the client too. That is what makes CSR so hugely powerful, and about far more than fundraising or volunteering.'"

Corporate Social Responsibility is a key component of the best long-term business strategies for companies of any size. Corporations must be ever mindful of the impact they have on the world in which we live. Understanding the immediacy of communications today and the impact they can have on your corporate brand means that CSR needs to be a fundamental part of your communications platform and your corporate DNA.

CHAPTER 14

Managing the Brand in a Merger

Merger Mania is Heating Up

SO WHAT DOES THAT MEAN FOR YOUR BRAND?

The banking crisis put a major damper on Merger & Acquisitions (M&A) activity. But cheap debt, plenty of cash in the corporate coffers, and a rising stock market can fuel hikes in merger activity. Does this mean you should be considering the acquisition of another company, or is it time to put your own firm on the block? Either way, if you move forward with a merger, it will have a major impact on your corporate brand.

Brands are often the last thing CEOs consider when they merge their company. Unfortunately, many executives learn how important the brand is to the value of the company only after they close the deal and start the process of putting the operations together.

Corporate mergers can often destroy corporate reputations that took years to build. When mergers fail to live up to expectations, all suffer: shareholders, employees, vendors, and, most importantly, customers — everyone associated with the merged companies. That is a key reason why careful consideration should be given to the anticipated brand strategy before any merger is concluded.

Brand Strategy from an M&A Perspective:

HOW WILL THE MERGER IMPACT YOUR EMPLOYEES?

Mergers typically create confusion, conflict, fear, anger, and uncertainty among employees. This leads to talent raiding, and competitors are often able to capture good people who are worried about their futures just when distracted executives need them the most.

HOW WILL THE COMPANIES BE INTEGRATED?

The integration process, or lack thereof, is often blamed for merger failures. A thoughtful and well-articulated 'Vision, Values, and Mission' statement for the newly combined entity will help sustain a positive tone for the merger and is something that should be created as part of the merger process rather than after the ink has dried.

WHAT WILL THE COMBINED COMPANIES BE CALLED?

Harried executives often consider the name of the company as an afterthought or with so much emotion that it evades logical thinking. The corporate brand is an important asset, and naming should be put on the negotiation table early in the merger process. An outside brand-consulting firm with brand valuation capabilities can offer alternative scenarios with the best naming recommendations and the potential value of each. My firm was consulted when communications giant SBC acquired AT&T. Management of the acquiring company naturally wanted SBC to be the new corporate name, but we concluded it would take billions of media dollars to elevate the SBC brand to the size and stature of the AT&T brand. Ed Whitacre, CEO, wisely chose the AT&T name for the combined entity.

EXPLOIT THE INITIAL INTEREST IN THE MERGER.

When you are ready to announce the merger, confirm that you are ready to exploit the initial interest in the newly formed company. There will never be a better chance to tell your story than in the initial thirty days; after that, the merger is old news. See that your senior spokespeople are trained on how to work with the media, and have your ad campaign and communications materials ready for release on the day of the announcement. Talk to the press. Be ready to announce to your investors the details of why this merger makes sense, make the most of your announcement.

DON'T FORGET BOTH SIDES OF THE ACQUISITION.

A budget for announcing and integrating communications of the newly merged entities should be established *before* the deal is concluded. This aspect of brand building is cost effective for protecting existing brand equity and building the merged brand.

Unfortunately, budgets are usually set *after* the deal is concluded. At that point, all the pressure focuses on cutting costs. Damage to the brand can be catastrophic if it is not properly funded immediately following a merger.

Merging the Cultures

You are not only merging the businesses but the cultures as well. Often this is the most difficult aspect of a merger. Communicate with consistency, communicate often, and communicate like you mean it. Tell your employees what kind of culture you are trying to build and how you expect them to behave. Get your employees involved in thinking about the new company with well-crafted purposeful brand workshops designed to create internal buy-in. Keeping your employees well informed about the merger and what to expect will help rebuild trust.

COMMUNICATIONS IS YOUR BEST TOOL.

Spend more time and resources than you think will be required to make the merger convincing. Utilize every communications vehicle to create excitement. It will take time, but communicating your new brand will pay big dividends.

There are always plenty of global economic headwinds that can quickly chill an M&A activity. If any of the global markets have a significant meltdown, it will likely domino and quickly cool off heated M&A markets. However, if you're looking for a merger, use your best brand resources to execute your plan.

MERGER & ACQUISITIONS: 1 + 1 = BETTER

Mergers and acquisitions are about making good brands better. Consider this maxim: When two brands merge, two fundamental truths emerge:

1) the acquiring company has the stronger balance sheet;

2) the acquired company has something that the bigger fish cannot otherwise get. Successful mergers are not games of sharks and minnows: they are strategic matches of mutual interest.

Brand valuation acumen is absolutely vital when two strong brands come under one corporate umbrella. The CEO relies on his or her senior management to assess the equity of both corporate brands in order to determine what aspects of each to retain or retire. What will the new organization look like? A quantitative market research program is imperative for engaging the leadership (as well as other key constituents) of both companies so that the M&A team can objectively assess brand strengths and weaknesses and develop a communication strategy that reassures internal and external audiences about the new combined enterprise.

CHAPTER 15

Are Corporate Brands Relevant in Today's Economy?

Tenet Partners' annual CoreBrand Top 100 BrandPower Rankings Report showcases the best and strongest corporate brands. The report analyzes the performance of brands throughout the past year as well as brand trends during the past five years. This ongoing study, combined with Tenet's CoreBrand Favorability Report, provides insight to better understand the dynamics that influence brand performance, and in time, this research helps separate the winners from the laggards. The lessons from these two studies are relevant for all businesses.

Both reports show that a well-managed brand can serve as a powerful business asset during flinty economic times as well as a tool to regain lost market share. Based on our research and findings, we distilled it into four key takeaways for leveraging your brand in today's market.

Build Your Relevance: Quantify Your Reputation Over Time.

It's difficult to stand out if you don't fundamentally understand what makes your company unique. Initiate research to justify your positioning and marketing activities, and engage tracking systems that help show successes of past initiatives and opportunities ahead. Understanding your strengths and weaknesses and how they match with audience needs and preferences clarifies what your needed and where your business should be moving.

When tracking your brand, it's important that your brand measurement program is not a single endeavor. Review this types of internal evaluation on a regular basis to determine if opportunities were taken or have changed and if threats have been overcome or new ones are on the horizon. At Tenet Partners, we encourage our clients to conduct these evaluations as frequently as quarterly or as far apart as annually because any less than that would make it difficult to pinpoint exactly what factor is responsible for success or failure.

Sustain Your Differentiation: Understand your competitors.

The purpose of your brand is to set you apart from the crowd and help buyers to understand your unique superiority. Being successfully differentiated is how to best utilize your blend of employees, products, and culture. Expand your research outwards to peers and competitors. This puts context to your actions when compared to that of your rivals and helps to highlight initiatives that you can take to better position yourself and stand out among the competition.

Sustain your differentiating relevance in the marketplace by clearly and proudly conveying your company's benefits and abilities. The stronger your claim on your position in the market, the greater impact your brand can have in attracting the right audiences.

Raise Your Credibility: Align your position for a solid reputation.

Align your messaging with current initiatives to ensure consumer trust in your efforts. It's not about how often you communicate, it's about strategically communicating to your target markets and defending your claims with actions. Talk is cheap when spoken but expensive when broken. Consumers are quick to backlash against broken promises or services that don't meet expectations. Building a brand isn't just about what you say – it's about what you do as well.

Use audience research and testing to refine brand messaging and ensure positive resonance with key targets. This requires time, perseverance, and dedication to growing positive sentiments toward the corporate brand, which feeds directly into growing brand Favorability.

Leverage Your Leaders: Putting your management where your mouth is.

During recent economic declines, we found that perceptions of management became more toxic than in past recessions. This indicates a level of mistrust and skepticism with leadership and underscores the critical role executives play in guiding brands through times of crisis. Audiences of all kinds look to leadership to build trust.

Senior management needs to promote clear, consistent, and transparent communications to the market. Set expectations by painting a vibrant picture of the vision for the company and the plan to achieve it. Lead by example, and show consumers that the company is well-rounded and focused on more than just profits.

While improving Familiarity is about highlighting your brand in appropriate ways, accelerating Favorability is about focusing on the quality of your brand messages.

CEOs who run the best performing companies understand where the company is today and where the potential to grow exists. These are the companies that are best positioned to take advantage of changing market conditions.

CHAPTER 16

Building Trust

Truth or Consequences

When did "Truth" lose its significance? Are there any "Consequences" for lying? Lies seem to be committed more and more frequently in politics and business with seemingly fewer consequences to those committing them. Somehow, it appears we have grown immune to the onslaught of falsehoods where truth simply doesn't matter anymore, and the ends justify the means.

Don't believe it. Truth matters, and you need to build it into the culture of your business, or the consequences can be devastating. Just like with the 1960s television show *Truth or Consequences*, I believe that the truth matters in business and in life. Trust with your customers is the most valuable of assets, and here are five ways to build trust into every business experience.

Building "Trust Points" into Every Business Experience

Most business leaders think of communications such as public relations, advertising, or packaging as the most obvious approaches to brand building. Trusted brands, however, are actually more efficiently and effectively built when brand alignment occurs among the business processes, the business culture, and ultimately the communications of a company and its products. Trust is built with every customer at every intersection of the brand experience. – Tenet Partners calls actively implemented, managed, and aligned communications that build brand confidence "trust points".

Here are five ways to build trust in your company.

#1 TRUST IS BUILT FROM THE FIRST INTERACTION.

Whether the interaction is intended or not, brand trust often begins with a potential customer's first interaction with the employees of a company. What is the first impression that is made? Is the employee knowledgeable, helpful, and friendly? If so, a trust point has been earned. Or does the body language say the employee is tired and would prefer not to have you in his life at that particular moment? In that case, unfortunately, a barrier to the brand has been created, and once the barrier is established, it takes much greater effort to overcome the resistance of the consumer to embrace the brand.

#2 MANAGING ALL TRUST POINTS WILL BUILD A BETTER BRAND.

Think about your favorite product or service. Every time you use that product, an impression is made. Ask yourself if the impression is positive, negative, or something in between. Consciously considering your own interactions with products you purchase will help you appreciate how consumers consider and grade your brand with every single interaction. Every trust point is an opportunity to build a lasting and positive impression with the brand.

#3 EVERY STAKEHOLDER HAS HIS OR HER OWN PERSPECTIVE.

Trust points are different for every constituency that is critical to a company's success. For example, the investor may consider consistent earnings the most important trust point. For employees, the trust point may be the employee salaries and benefits offered by the company. For the customer, the quality and price of the products or services are the most significant components of trust. What all these stakeholders have in common is a desire to be treated with respect, which is the essence of trust.

#4 INTANGIBLE ASSETS HAVE TANGIBLE VALUE.

Building trust creates a premium value for product brands as well as enterprise value for the corporate brand. While accounting standards don't yet justify brand value on the balance sheet, we know it plays a significant role in efficiently building businesses. In other words, it takes less of an investment to sell your products if you are a trusted company.

#5 CONSISTENT BEHAVIOR BUILDS TRUST.

Trust is built over many different dimensions depending on the perspective of the stakeholder constituency. Having a clear vision that your employees are trained to communicate consistently over time is the best way to build brand trust and value.

Likewise, truth is simply good for business. It builds trust, and trust creates value. Customers want to buy from companies they can trust. Investors want to invest in companies they trust. The media would like to write articles about companies who give them the straight scoop. Employees want to work for a company that is trustworthy.

When lies are told in business or in politics, there should be consequences, and much is revealed about the decline of our society and culture if lying becomes the norm and truth the casualty.

Celebrity Endorsements – A Good Idea Riddled with Pitfalls

Many marketers think that seeking a celebrity endorsement is a good way to build quickly and efficiently the trust in a brand. There is no doubt that associating your brand with a rising star celebrity can increase awareness of your brand with certain audiences. However, there are many pitfalls that should be considered before pursuing this approach.

A few months before he passed away, I had the opportunity to meet and have lunch with someone I have most admired in business during my career: Fred DeLuca, Founder and CEO, Subway, who took a concept and a $1,000 investment from a family friend and built it into one of the largest fast food franchises in history. Fred's personal story is a fascinating one, but it is the story he told me about the now infamous Jared Fogel, former spokesperson for the Subway brand, that is most intriguing.

When Jared was in college, his mother sent Fred a letter of how Jared's primarily eating Subway sandwiches helped him lose a significant amount of weight. Fred said that he shared the letter with the Subway marketing team but couldn't get any real interest for developing Jared's experiences into an advertising concept.

When Fred received a second letter from Jared's mother, he became more adamant about coercing the marketing team to become engaged in the idea of a spokesperson for the company. After some testing that showed the concept resonated with consumers, "Jared" was launched, and what a ride it was. The company grew significantly with a cohesive and compelling national advertising campaign. Subway also had succeeded in making Jared a celebrity.

As for Jared the person – all he had to do was to behave. Human nature being what it is, it has a tendency to make this relatively easy goal insurmountable for some people, and that is the precise problem with celebrity endorsements.

It wasn't long ago that Tiger Woods was a pristine celebrity endorser who commanded the highest prices for his endorsements, but when his infidelity with a number of women came into the spotlight, he lost the support of Accenture, General Motors, Gillette, and Gatorade. The notable exception that stayed with Tiger was Nike Golf, which had built their golf division around him.

Another celebrity endorser of the highest caliber was Bill Cosby, who played for so many years the squeaky clean, funny, and wise Dr. Cliff Huxtable on the Cosby Show. Who would have ever thought the investment in associating Bill Cosby with your product would be a risk? Yet for companies like Coke, Jell-O, Ford, etc., his celebrity asset became a liability when accusations of his sexual wrongdoing came to light.

Investing in celebrity endorsements in this world of social media seems to have multiplied the flawed exposure that can instantaneously transition a tweet or an Instagram into an embarrassment with the potential to activate enormous financial pain for the unwary marketer.

So is getting a celebrity to endorse your product worth the cost, and equally important but often less considered, is it worth the trust risk to your brand? No doubt the borrowed interest of a celebrity can help you build brand familiarity and awareness if the product and the celebrity are a good match. But beyond the significant investment, you should ask if the celebrity's endorsement power is diluted – or, put another way, has this individual spread his fame over so many products that he might confuse the public about his genuine belief in the product being endorsed? The more products sanctioned by a celebrity, the weaker the association with your brand.

Here is a checklist of considerations for using a celebrity to advocate your brand:

Is there a logical and natural fit between the celebrity and your brand?

What is it that gave your endorser celebrity status? Is it compatible with attributes you want to be associated with your brand?

Consider that the celebrity also wants to be associated with attributes that will promote his/her own career – take the time to understand *his/her* brand.

Some celebrities have the potential of overwhelming your brand that results in consumers' recalling the celebrity but not your brand.

If your celebrity is carrying too many endorsements, it will dilute your brand's distinctiveness.

Make sure your audience will associate the celebrity with your brand. Don't trust your instincts on this – trust your research.

You need to budget enough marketing dollars for both the celebrity and the media. Hiring celebrities has the potential to put you into the big leagues, but it will cost you. If you want to test the celebrity waters without breaking the bank, consider hiring the celebrity for a limited social media campaign.

Make sure any celebrity endorsement contract includes a good-conduct morality clause. This simply protects the brand from unexpected acts that would tend to cause hurt or embarrassment in any way. This is so important even when you believe there isn't a remote possibility that this particular celebrity would do anything foolish to damage his career or your brand. Subway wisely ended its association with Jared no doubt by invoking such a clause. History shows even the best celebrities are human.

CHAPTER 17

Entrepreneurship — Not All Brands Are Big

Selling your Personal Brand

FIFTEEN LESSONS FOR INDIVIDUALS AND ENTREPRENEURS

I was asked by University of South Florida Dean Moez Limayem to speak to the Executive MBA class about the subject of "Selling Your Personal Brand." We actually sell ourselves every day of our lives in ways that we are not even aware of, but we are never taught how to do this. I was thrilled to take on the assignment.

As I worked on my talk, I realized how closely personal branding and corporate branding parallel each other. I've always said, and you've seen it numerous times in this book, "Corporate reputation is the result of everything the corporation says and does, whether it's intended or not." The same exact statement can be made about personal reputation which is the perception of you by those who matter the most. What they perceive is the long term accumulation of your actions and comments.

Selling your personal brand means you have to organize it in a way so that it can create over time positive cumulative impressions. It takes thinking about your personal brand and creating guardrails for maintaining the image that reflects the true you!

Having no history of managing personal brands, I decided to take a fresh look at my own life, how I arrived at this point, and where I plan to take my life. It was quite an interesting exercise, and here are the fifteen key lessons I've learned about building a personal brand:

#1 YOU CAN LET EVENTS DEFINE YOU... or you can define the events! Life can throw you some curve balls that may surprise you, but if you have an overall plan for your life, then your chances of a successful path are much greater.

#2 ASSESS YOURSELF. You are one of seven billion people on earth. There is a mass of competition.

#3 DIFFERENTIATE YOURSELF TO STAND OUT FROM THE CROWD. If you've ever had to evaluate a stack of resumes, you know they quickly start to look the same. Stand out from the crowd! If your accomplishments alone are not enough, use a photo or different colored paper to help get attention.

#4 SET AUDACIOUS GOALS. You'll achieve them faster than you know. When I got out of college, I set two outrageously large goals: to go to New York and to open an advertising agency on Madison Avenue. I accomplished both by the time I was twenty-three years old (albeit a small agency).

#5 DON'T LISTEN TO THE NAYSAYERS. Live your dream. There will be plenty of friends and family who, with the best of intentions, will discourage you from seeking your goals. Remember these are *your* goals.

#6 SEEK A LIFE PARTNER WHO SHARES YOUR VISION. Love is great, but when you have a partner who understands and shares your vision, then great things can happen even faster!

#7 BE PREPARED FOR CHANGE. Resistance is futile. The world is changing at a very fast pace. What you learn in college is less important than how you learn because life and work change continuously.

#8 BE FORGIVING OF YOUR OWN MISTAKES. Everyone makes mistakes. Recognize them, correct what you can, and move on. Don't dwell on mistakes because it wastes valuable time.

#9 NEVER BE A GENERALIST. It will doom your growth. Focus on a specialization that is in demand or will be in demand in the future.

#10 DEVELOP A FLEXIBLE PERSONAL BUSINESS STRATEGY. When your goals evolve, take the time to fine-tune your strategy of life. Keep adjusting and resetting based on the circumstances you face.

#11 DO SOMETHING IMPOSSIBLE. Seek the Holy Grail of your industry. If you really want to stand out from everyone else, solve an unsolvable problem. Take the time to think about it, and the solution might surprise you.

#12 WRITING BOOKS AND GIVING SPEECHES WILL PUT YOU ON THE MAP. I was never a particularly good writer, and I was deathly afraid to give speeches. Understanding and communications training helped me on the path to success. I became good at both. Face your fears, and it will pay dividends.

#13 GIVE BACK TO THE COMMUNITY. Some of the best clients I've landed were met when I was helping the nonprofit community or serving on the board of a nonprofit organization. Never underestimate the value of giving back.

#14 RECOGNIZE MILESTONES. It pays to celebrate milestones in life because it is a recognition of where you are on the path of life and your career.

#15 PLAN YOUR EXIT STRATEGY. If you know when and how you plan to retire, it will help you prepare for that exit before you zoom past it.

Renaissance of Enterprise

The future is bright for individuals looking to become entrepreneurs.

Many companies are trailblazing new and resourceful paths to differentiate themselves as brands and to succeed as businesses. There are fascinating and innovative marketplace trends emerging.

Trends to Watch:

BOOTSTRAPPING & ENTREPRENEURIAL RESURGENCE

American business is rolling up its sleeves. The whole country is ready to get things done the old fashioned way – by bootstrapping. Bootstrapping is "having less financing costs and finding alternative resources to achieve success." Established companies with thin resources are seeking out new and innovative ways to finance their enterprises, and startups are doing it as a way to launch new ventures.

THE RISE OF CROWDFUNDING IN MAINSTREAM FUNDING

The traditional banking system, which has historically been the finance engine for small business, has faded as a resource for funding. This funding vacuum has given entrepreneurs the impetus to seek out innovative methods to finance new ventures. Crowdfunding through social media will become more sophisticated and mainstream in the future and will be a key catalyst for fueling innovative ideas. The breakthroughs of crowdfunding will have everyone from investment bankers to entrepreneurs rethinking how to finance and scale growth.

THE SCALABILITY OF THE COLLABORATIVE ECONOMY

The collaborative economy is an expanding growth innovation that is emerging in the technology and business services sectors. New partnerships and alliances are being fueled out of necessity – as it is simply an effective path to success. Today's technologies provide entrepreneurs with new product creation and resource sharing abilities to network and find solutions rather than use precious funds on equipment and people.

EMERGENCE OF "LOCAL" ARTISANS

On the heels of a sluggish economy, we are seeing an emergence of local uprisings on many levels. This concept is now appearing in consumer goods. The rise of artisanal brands will increase in the US, and there will be more varieties of brands in categories once dominated by giant companies (liquor, beer, soft drinks) spawned by startups with a "local" feel. There is something inherently American about this leading-edge trend driven by consumers supporting "organic" and "local" initiatives. Technologies and online forums will continue to fuel the momentum of these startups at a significantly higher rate.

INCREASE IN CUSTOMER INTERACTION AND HONESTY

Consumers have more communications power than ever, and they demand answers. There will be an increase in direct interaction between companies and their customers through social media (comments, product changes, customer input). This will put pressure on companies to be more authentic in marketing and focus on honesty about ingredients, processes, and benefits of the products. Honesty will be the power behind marketing moving forward.

CONVERGENCE OF THE PHYSICAL AND DIGITAL EXPERIENCES

Physical and digital interactions are merging across a wide spectrum. Smartphones are delivering data while you shop or watch TV. Tablets are letting you interact with television in real time. Conferences will focus on gathering and transmitting streams of data while hosting live audiences and speaker forums. This convergence of physical and digital is also taking place in real-time manufacturing. While 3D printing has been available for decades, the process is becoming more sophisticated while owning a 3D printer is becoming less expensive. This technology is quickly evolving from rapid prototyping to mass customization manufacturing.

CONTENT-DRIVEN MARKETING AND COMMUNICATIONS

Consumer influence will continue to evolve the role of business marketing and communications. Chief Marketing Officers (CMO) will become even more engaged in the business operations to better face the ever changing challenges. Content takes a seat at the head of the branding table as a key value proposition on how companies engage with customers. Customers will seek more information than ever before through all channels and become more thoroughly educated before moving to an action/outcome.

BIG DATA IS NO LONGER A BUZZWORD

"Big Data" will continue to be mined to seek deeper and deeper consumer insights for product development, marketing, and sales. The CMO's role will become more influential than that of the Chief Information Officer (CIO) because of the CMO's need to embrace and leverage "Small Data" (contextualized Big Data) to grow revenue and enterprise value. As this trend develops, the CMO's tenure will lengthen, and the career path will ultimately lead to the next generation of CEOs.

BRAND STEWARDSHIP ISN'T GONE

Corporate America has indeed joined the "warm and fuzzy" bandwagon – a very positive development. Corporate Social Responsibility (CSR) and sustainability programs will continue attracting board level attention in major companies. Employees, communities, media, customers, and shareholders are raising expectations about the role of corporations to take and maintain a leadership position in implementing high-level CSR and sustainable standards.

THE OVERALL OUTLOOK FOR THE US IS DECIDEDLY UPBEAT

For the first time in decades, the US is realizing a lower cost of domestic energy. When combined with a drive for success among its workforce, new innovations, lower borrowing, and marketing costs, the US will become even more competitive globally with its manufacturing efforts. By keeping costs in line, more consumers will be seeking out American-made products.

Enthusiasm for Global Entrepreneurism

A few years ago, I took a Harvard Business School course on entrepreneurism. I have never been in a place with so many like-minded individuals from every corner of the globe. We were all entrepreneurs, and we were energized!

I was also amazed by how these individuals from around the world were attuned to our culture – "Americanized" as one attendee described it. They seemed to know everything that was going on in our national news from politics to sports to fashion. They also respected America's culture of capitalism and free enterprise, which is something not herd often in the media since business and corporate leaders are so often demonized. Even Hollywood often poses the businessman as the bad guy.

American entrepreneurs and the startup companies they create are critical to healthy economic growth, but the annual number of startup companies has been falling for decades.

The Kauffman Foundation, citing its own research and drawing on US Census data, concluded that the number of companies less than a year old had declined as a share of all businesses by nearly 44 percent between 1978 and 2012. (The Vanishing, Leigh Buchanan, INC., May 2015)

These entrepreneurs at Harvard came to learn about entrepreneurism and plant the seed of capitalism in their own country and culture. Now, I'm borrowing a seed from them to replant it here. That seed is "Enthusiasm for Entrepreneurism." I believe as they did – entrepreneurism is a universal language that can solve many of the world's economic woes.

After learning that I had been an entrepreneur for decades, one of the participants asked me for the advice I would give someone who had a burning desire to become an entrepreneur but wasn't entirely sure if he had the necessary expertise or qualities to be successful. I developed ten questions that should be considered before making the decision.

So You Want to Be an Entrepreneur?

If you think you are an entrepreneur, answer these questions to be sure.

#1 WHAT ARE YOUR PASSIONS? THIS IS WHAT GETS YOU EXCITED.

List all of them and rank them in order of preference

#2 ARE THERE CAREER OPPORTUNITIES IN ANY AREA OF ANY YOUR PASSIONS?

Yes/No – if "no" is the answer then go to the next passion

#3 WHAT IS YOUR BEST CAREER PATH?

Staff position/Entrepreneur – which one is the quickest path to success?

#4 WHAT IS THE TOP POSITION ATTAINABLE IN YOUR AREA OF INTEREST?

Make that your ultimate career goal

#5 IS THERE A BURNING PLATFORM IN THIS AREA (SOMETHING THAT EVERYONE SAYS CAN'T BE ACCOMPLISHED) THAT YOU BELIEVE YOU CAN ACHIEVE?

Make this your vision

#6 CAN YOU DEVELOP THIS INTO A FIVE-YEAR POINT OF DIFFERENTIATION?

This becomes the mission

#7 WHAT WILL IT TAKE TO LEVERAGE THIS POINT OF DIFFERENTIATION?

Your process becomes the start of a business plan

#8 WHAT ARE THE OBSTACLES TO YOUR SUCCESS?

Be honest, write them down, plan to solve them one by one

#9 WHAT AFFILIATIONS DO YOU NEED TO MAKE TO SUCCEED?

List them and start to make those contacts (e.g. PR professional, banker, potential partners, etc.)

#10 WHO ARE THE INDIVIDUALS CRITICAL TO YOUR SUCCESS?

Identify and nurture constantly contacts that can make a difference at key points along your growth path

Entrepreneurship may not be as appealing as it was in past decades, but there is hope, and there are many new opportunities at hand for aspiring entrepreneurs. Universities are offering more courses on entrepreneurism. There are many glowing success stories of entrepreneurs reinventing and disrupting older business models and industries. The tech-sector is virtually booming with startups. New financing methods such as crowdfunding are a viable and growing alternative to traditional banking. The aspiring entrepreneur only needs to do what comes naturally – ***START!***

CHAPTER 18

Clear, Concise, and Consistent Communications

What are the Keys to Success in Branding?

I am often asked to identify the most essential fail-safe elements of brand building. My advice is always the same: If you do nothing else but communicate clearly and consistently over time a concise message, then you will have done more to build your brand than the vast majority of existing companies. We call that message the "brand directive," and it should show up in everything you say and do.

One of the most common failures in marketing communications comes when management gets bored with its own message and alters it at the very point when the message is starting to become effective. We call this "message fatigue," and it is one of the most wasteful aspects of branding.

So what do clear, concise, and consistent communications actually mean?

CLEAR – The brand strategy follows the business strategy and should be communicated so there is no ambiguity about the strategic intent and direction of management. Remember that the brand strategy is the communicated business strategy.

CONCISE – If you can boil down the brand directive into a sentence or two, that is ideal. It should not be more than a few sentences and does not have to be as pithy as a slogan to be effective. It is usually a better use of your time to communicate the concept and let your branding firm or advertising agency fine-tune it into a slogan or tag line.

CONSISTENT –Consistently stick to the message over time so that it has an impact. Consistency is not just about communications – your message should be reflected in everything you say and do as a leader and as a company.

COMMUNICATIONS – Communications is more than the verbal and printed word. It also includes intended communication such as advertising and public relations and unintended communications such as an open microphone capturing a conversation that is not for public consumption. It is literally everything your business says and does. Therefore, managing communications is a very important job, and it applies to every person in the company.

The other element that needs to be considered is:

OVER TIME – While we recommend sticking to a message for the long term, in reality, we recognize that everything will eventually require periodic refreshing. Rather than relying on gut instinct to determine the best time to refresh your brand, we believe it is wise to do periodic third-party benchmark tracking research with your key stakeholders to evaluate how your brand is impressing those who are most important to your brand. Some of those key stakeholders are investors, employees, customers, media, community, and social networks. While this research can be done internally, we have found that using an outside third party is much more likely to yield the most forthright answers regarding decisions around your brand.

An example of a clear brand directive in three simple words is "Truth Well Told" – the credo for the global advertising agency McCann Erickson, which is a division of Interpublic Group of Companies. These three words say so much about the clarion call for the classic advertising agency, and it has stood the test of time since the agency's founding in 1912.

Johnson & Johnson's famous company credo "challenges us [the employees] to put the needs and well-being of the people we serves *first*." When J&J's credo was tested in early 2011 by a few misguided management decisions resulting in a number of product recalls, the resulting misalignment of the brand was so clear and jarring that the company quickly identified and corrected the path and the declining trajectory of this otherwise stalwart brand. You would know by gut instinct that something was wrong, but quantitative research confirmed it and took the emotion out of the discussion.

"You're in good hands with Allstate" is a tagline and a promise introduced in 1956. It says all you need to know about this insurance company and does it in a timeless manner. It says that you are smart to do business with Allstate since it will take care of your needs.

All three examples above have withstood the test of time and are as relevant today as when they were created.

"Clear, concise, and consistent communications" is a touchstone for all your branding efforts. Always make sure your investments in brand building meet these criteria, and you will stay ahead of the competition.

CONCLUSION

Corporate Brand Value

Measure, Maintain, Nurture, and Protect

Corporate Brand Value is your corporate crown jewel. We believe it is as important to the enterprise value as human resources, capital resources, secret recipes, real estate, or manufacturing and logistical infrastructure.

Great companies put in place systematic methods for evaluating and improving their brand's familiarity, coherence, and reputation. These methods provide tremendous insight for senior managers and C-suite executives into their brand's strengths and weaknesses. Systematic evaluation leads the way to clear, concise, and enduring brand management that is made visible through clear, concise, and consistent brand-building campaigns and manifested through improved shareholder value. It's that simple.

How Do You Measure Brand Value?

Like a diamond, the best brands sparkle and shine, drawing attention, admiration, and sometimes –envy. While color, carat, clarity, and cut are the 4 Cs of the gem industry, companies may be measured by these five indices: familiarity, coherence, favorability, leadership, and investment worthiness.

FAMILIARITY (RECOGNITION) – How well is your brand recognized by key constituents?

COHERENCE – How coherent is your brand? Do others recognize its breadth and depth? Is that perception an accurate reflection of your brand's whole story?

FAVORABILITY (REPUTATION) – What do others think of your company's human resources, products, and services? What is its reputation?

LEADERSHIP – How do key constituents view the quality of your corporate and brand leadership? Do they view its leadership as transparent and accountable? Do they respect its integrity? Do they admire its operation and vision?

INVESTMENT WORTHINESS – Does the financial community view your corporation and its brands as appealing investments?

Tenet's CoreBrand Index® is a proven brand evaluation tool. It is used to show the correlation between brand equity and overall financial performance. Investments in brand building can be determined, implemented, evaluated, and adjusted to meet target ROI.

We at Tenet Partners know that no two companies are exactly alike, but we have demonstrated again and again that corporations must establish a standard set of metrics and reporting methods to determine the value of their brand and to identify specific strategies required to make that brand shine with the color, clarity, and carat of a diamond.

After all, who wants their corporate brand to be an insignificant sparkle around the neck? You want your brand to be as legendary as the 317 carat Second Star of Africa on the Imperial State Crown of Great Britain: brilliant and big, dazzling and clear, front and center.

Great brands are your Corporate Crown Jewels. Measure them. Maintain them. Nurture them. Protect them. Share them with the world.

CONCLUSION 153

The Second Star of Africa, White Diamond,
Front and Center, Above the Ermine, Closest to the Queen

ALSO BY JAMES R. GREGORY

The Patent Book
How to Protect and Market Your Ideas

Marketing Corporate Image
The Company as Your Number One Product

Leveraging the Corporate Brand

Branding Across Borders
A Guide to Global Brand Marketing

The Best of Branding
Best Practices in Corporate Branding

Made in the USA
San Bernardino, CA
17 February 2017